EVERY WORD AN ARROW

LEONA SILBERBERG

Every Word an Arrow

Copyright © 2015 by Leona Silberberg

ISBN 978-0-9860994-0-3

This novel is dedicated to everyone who has ever found themselves at the mercy of the divorce industry and the family court system.

Acknowledgments

I want to acknowledge the help of my friends in California, Montana, Utah, New Mexico and Canada. I especially want to thank Lisa for urging me to write this book and my mother for her unwavering support.

A thick flurry of snowflakes drifted weightlessly from the sky, blanketing the historic buildings and streets of Josie's hometown. Adorned with wreaths and red holiday bows, the vintage street lamps cast a yellow glow on the swirling downy snow. It was early evening on the day of the monthly gallery walk in this college town in the Northern Rockies, and the first big storm of the season had just blown into town. The downtown art galleries were serving hot spiced wine and cookies, while groups of locals, mostly college students and hipsters, made the rounds, met up with friends and checked out the artwork. The atmosphere was festive. Finals week at the university was over and Christmas vacation had just begun.

Josie stood at the edge of the crowd and gazed out the window. Her seven-year-old son, Austen, was outside with his best friend, catching snowflakes on his tongue and jumping in waist-high piles of snow. A young couple from one of her classes kissed briefly, before stomping the snow off their boots and entering the gallery hand in hand.

About two dozen people squeezed into the former fly-fishing shop, which her friends had just finished renovating into an art gallery. Small and bright, it was well situated, around the corner from the big galleries with just enough space to showcase her work. The single paragraph review in the following day's paper said turnout for her show had been good for a new artist, and that was true, even if many of the people who turned out were her friends, neighbors and former students.

After smoothing her dress against her slim figure, Josie ran her fingers nervously through her wavy shoulder length hair. Tall and leggy, she was more confident and attractive at forty-three than she had been in years. Suddenly, a hand clasped her shoulder and she turned around to see Iggy, warm and exuberant as usual.

"You're a rock star – look at this crowd!" he said, his mass of curly blond hair falling out of his cap and his dazzling smile set on high beam. "The work is great! Everyone loves it!"

"Thanks, Iggy. I was worried that the subject matter would be too heavy for a lot of people," Josie said, gesturing towards a painting of a nude woman with a snake wrapped around her torso. "But, it was the imagery that came to me and I just went with it. I was tempted to call it my 'Big D' show."

Francine, the ultimate hipster babe, waved from across the room and Josie made her way over there, giving her twelve-year-old daughter Phoebe a quick hug on the way.

"Wow, Francine, can you believe this? So much has happened since I met you four years ago, and now here we are at my opening – I still can't get my head around it." Josie glanced at her phone to check the time and realized it was the sixth of December – her own personal independence day and exactly five years since her marriage had abruptly and irrevocably ended.

"I love this piece – it's mysterious and evocative," Francine enthused. A striking woman in her early thirties with thick auburn hair and an athlete's body, Francine was wearing a long purple vintage dress draped with faux pearls.

"Thanks, Francine, I think it's my best work. I almost hope it doesn't sell because I'd be sad to see it go."

The two women stood before a large painting hanging by itself on the back wall of the gallery. The scene depicted a massive bull elk standing in a clearing with an unconscious nude woman draped in his antlers. The image was both frightening and mystical. Francine's husband, Beau, walked over and put an arm around his wife.

"Where do you come up with these images?" he asked Josie. "They're wild."

∽ 2 ∾

The elk was a perfect specimen – the sort of animal that hunters throughout Montana dream of taking. He was at least eight-hundred pounds of muscle and brawn, with antlers that spread out over five feet in width and another four feet in height. He stepped carefully and deliberately into a clearing in the brush, and took in his surroundings.

Surreal and unexpected, there was a woman draped languidly over his twisted and velvet-covered antlers, her arms and legs dangling limply. She was unconscious, and oblivious to her precarious situation. Slowly, the regal and magnificent beast bent his head forward and forcefully stomped one of his front hooves against the ground. The woman didn't move. He bent lower and jerked his head, visibly jostling the sleeping woman. Still, she remained unconscious. Finally, the bull bent down one last time – deep enough to throw the woman off his horns completely and into the thorns and bramble below. Just as he thrust his head forward to launch her into her fate, Josie woke up.

She sat up in bed and heard two loud thumps against the wall and the sound of a child screaming. It was just past midnight and she'd been asleep for less than an hour. Her husband, Richard, yelled "Go to bed," and slammed the door to his office.

Josie got out of bed and went into the hallway. Her daughter, Phoebe, then seven years old, sat crumpled on the floor sobbing. "Daddy hurt me. Mommy, Daddy hurt me." Josie put her arms around her crying child and pulled her to her feet. She gently walked Phoebe into her purple and green butterfly-festooned bedroom. "I just wanted my blankey. I left it in the living room. Daddy said I couldn't get it. He hurt me. I hate Daddy."

"Okay, sweetie, just stay here. I'll get your blankey." Josie settled Phoebe on the bed and walked through the empty, lifeless rooms of her large suburban California Bay Area home. She felt like crying too, but she never did. So many times her daughter had said to her 'I hate Daddy.' Usually she replied without thinking, "No you don't sweetie, Daddy loves you." So many times she'd come running from some other part of the house at the sound of Phoebe screaming and Richard yelling.

When a neighbor recently remarked that she'd heard Phoebe say she hated her father, Josie had brushed it off. "All kids hate their parents. It's totally normal," she'd told the neighbor.

Her neighbor shook her head and said "maybe teenagers hate their parents, but I've heard Phoebe say that since she was two and that's not normal. I just thought you should know."

Josie shuddered, picked up the ragged baby blanket from the floor and headed back to her daughter's room. Phoebe was holding her head and sniffling. She grabbed her blanket from Josie, rolled it up into a ball and hugged it to her chest.

"Okay, Phoebe, let me look at your head." Josie sat next to Phoebe and gently moved her hand away from her head. She carefully felt for any swelling. "Does it still hurt?" She asked.

"It still hurts a little. Daddy pushed me against the wall."

"I know, sweetie, I heard the thumps. I don't feel any swelling so I think you'll be okay, but I'll stay up with you for a while just to be sure."

Josie rocked Phoebe in her arms and entertained her with another chapter of their made up story about Otterella, the otter who lives in the Russian River and her best friend, Rushika, the Russian girl who lives in an eighteenth-century fort nearby and tries to save the otters from being killed for their skins. The story of Otterella and Rushika was Phoebe's all-time favorite because she'd made up the names herself when they were at their family cabin on the Russian River one weekend. It was the one story guaranteed to keep Phoebe awake and riveted, and Josie needed to keep her awake for an hour as a precaution since she'd hit her head.

After she tucked Phoebe into bed, Josie went down the hall to Richard's office. She entered without knocking. He was shutting down the computer and putting away his files. "What happened?" she asked, quietly closing the door behind her.

"What do you mean?" Richard replied, not bothering to look up.

"I mean, I woke up and I heard you yelling. I heard Phoebe crying. I heard the sound of her head getting knocked against the wall. Phoebe said you pushed her and you hurt her."

"I told her to go to bed. It was midnight." Richard shrugged. "She accidentally fell against the wall when she was going to her room."

"I don't believe you. You pushed her. You know she gets scared if she doesn't have her blanket. Why did you do it? Why did you hurt her?" Josie was trying to keep her voice low.

Richard got up from his chair and walked up close to his wife. At six feet even he was just an inch taller than her, but he outweighed her by at least thirty pounds. He glared into her eyes and she took a step back.

"Richard, we can't go on like this. This is child abuse. You can't keep hurting these kids." He leaned in closer. His eyes, intense and angry, had transformed from to their usual green to storm cloud gray. He was a different person now. He wasn't the man she'd married. He was mad so often lately that she'd half-jokingly began referring to him as the 'madman.'

Ironically, he was the one who wanted to have kids right away. He was ten years older than her, and talked her into getting pregnant less than a year after the wedding. As much as he wanted kids, he became a different person after they were born.

"I don't care if you believe me. She fell and hurt herself. I didn't hurt her, and even if I did you can't prove it." He glared daggers at her. Josie stepped aside and he left the room.

Richard had the same response every time she confronted him about this issue: 'you can't prove it.' One time when he was playing a game he called 'daddy monster' with their toddler son, Austen, he shoved a door in Austen's face and caused a bruise. He said it was an accident and Josie accepted it.

She chose to believe Richard in the past, because she was committed to her marriage and couldn't fathom the idea of getting divorced. Divorce was an alien world to her. Divorce was rare in her large extended family, and she'd be an outcast if she divorced. She also didn't want to think about the financial implications of divorce. Socially and financially, divorce felt like nothing short of Armageddon to Josie, but she could no longer deny that her children were being traumatized and abused.

She slumped down onto the couch in Richard's office and closed her eyes. The dream came back. The elk was trying to tell her something. He was trying to wake her up. He was trying to help her. She'd been unconscious for too long. She had been willfully avoiding seeing what was right before her. She had refused to open her eyes and see the situation for what it was: she'd married an abuser and now she would have to risk everything she'd worked so hard for in order to protect her children and give them a happy childhood. She put her hands to her face but the tears wouldn't come. She was the figure in the dream and she was caught on the horns of a dilemma.

∞ 3 ∞

Twenty-three separate stacks of paper and a pile of manila envelopes were laid out in front of Josie as she settled in to her weekly volunteer job in Phoebe's second-grade classroom. Austen sat quietly on the floor next to her feet playing 'zoom zoom' with his cars while Phoebe's teacher, Ms. Larson, was busy on her computer across the room. It was Wednesday afternoon, and Josie was organizing school work to put into the Friday folders. Phoebe was outside on the playground honing her already formidable skill on the rings. It was a beautiful December afternoon in Josie's East Bay suburb, and the classroom door was propped open. Shouts and laughter drifted in from the playground.

Ms. Larson looked up and said "Mrs. Bain, I would like to speak with you when you have a minute."

"No problem, Ms. Larson." Josie went over and sat on the small plastic chair next to the teacher's desk. Austen was busy racing his cars across the floor.

"I need to talk to you about something that came up with Phoebe today. During morning recess she said something to me that I felt should be reported to the principal."

"Oh, what did she say?" Josie asked, suddenly feeling queasy.

"She said her Daddy hurts her. I asked her to describe what he did and she said he hits her and he shoves and yells at her all the time. Is that true, Mrs. Bain?"

"Well, I know something is wrong, but he never does anything when I'm there except yell at her. I'm always out of the room and then I hear Phoebe crying and him yelling. Sometimes she's on the floor and it seems like he may have hit her or pushed her, but he always says she fell by herself." Josie started feeling hot, despite the cool fall temperature.

"Mrs. Bain, I need you to know that I'm a mandated reporter and I had no choice but to report what Phoebe told me. She was interviewed by the principal today, and I was informed that a case worker from Child Protective Services was also present."

"Wow," Josie said, her head starting to spin. "I don't know what to say and I don't know what to do."

"You can't tolerate that behavior towards Phoebe. It's child abuse and if you continue to tolerate it, you're as guilty as he is," Ms. Larson said sharply.

"Okay, I know. I am just starting to realize that myself. You're right of course. It's just that I need time to figure this out – I need time to make a plan." Josie slumped in her chair.

"There is no time, Mrs. Bain. CPS has been called, they interviewed Phoebe, and now there will be an investigation." Ms. Larson paused, and then softened her tone. "Do you have any brothers? Anyone who can help you? Your husband has to move out of the house."

"He'll never move. I know he'll never move. We bought the house together before Phoebe was born, but he sees it as his house and I know he'll never leave it. He's worked on it a lot. He put the hardwood floors in by himself. He remodeled the kitchen. And as for my brothers – they're both busy and they don't live around here anyway. My dad died last year. I really don't have anyone to help me." Josie blinked back a tear. Talking about her dad still choked her up.

Ms. Larson leaned forward, and gently touched Josie's hand. "Okay, Mrs. Bain, I'll explain to you what you need to do. You need to go to court and get a restraining order against him and force him to move out. There are several different courts – you need to go to the family court, which I believe is two blocks west of the traffic court downtown. Have you ever been to traffic court?"

"No," Josie said softly. "I've never been in a courthouse in my life for any reason."

"Well, you'll have to look up the address for the family court. Then you need to write down everything you can remember about any of the times he may have hit Phoebe. Write down any of the times you heard her crying and heard him yelling at her – even if you didn't see it happen. Make a log. It has to be specific – time, date, place."

"Take the log to the courthouse with you," Ms. Larson continued. "And bring a friend. You'll have to fill out paperwork for a temporary restraining order and attach a copy of the log. When you get the signed order back, you need to find your husband and have your friend hand him the order. You need to act soon – preferably today - tomorrow at the latest."

Josie stood abruptly, knocking over the tiny chair. "Today? I have to do this today? This is all happening too fast. I'm in shock. I worked with a guy once who had a restraining order against him. We all knew what he was like. He drank and got into fights. I could totally see him hitting his wife. Richard isn't like that. He never hit me. I can't believe I have to go to court and get a restraining order. We're not that kind of people." She felt sick.

"I'm sorry, Mrs. Bain. He may not have hit you, but he is hitting Phoebe. It is your job to protect the children or CPS has the right to take them away from you. If it makes you feel any better, I had to go to court once and get a restraining order against my boyfriend. It happens. It happens to people you would never suspect." Ms. Larson leaned back in her chair.

"Mrs. Bain, I'll take care of the Friday folders. You have a lot on your plate right now."

"Okay, thanks Ms. Larson." Josie gathered her things, took Austen by the hand and left the room.

Richard walked in the door upbeat and cheerful that evening – as if nothing had happened. He put his briefcase on the table and sat down to take off his shoes.

"We need to talk." Josie sat down next to him.

"I'm tired. We can talk later." Richard waved her off as he went into his office. Undeterred, Josie followed him in and closed the door behind her.

"No, this is important. We need to talk now. We've been reported to Child Protective Services. They want to interview us. They've started an investigation." Richard stared hard at Josie, suddenly giving her his full attention.

"What did you do now, Josie?" He raised his voice. "Did you go and tell a bunch of lies to get me in trouble? You won't get away with it. This is the biggest mistake you've ever made." Richard glared at her as the veins on his neck pulsated with anger.

"You have to believe me. I didn't do anything. I went to school today and Phoebe's teacher told me. Phoebe is seven years old. She's not a little baby. She is very intelligent. She told her teacher everything. The school reported it. I'm just trying to figure out what to do." Josie started to raise her voice.

"And you're not making it any easier. You have to move out. There is no other option. You can go to your family until this gets sorted out. If you don't move out they can take the kids away," Josie yelled, no longer caring if the kids could hear her.

"The only place I have to go is back to Montana, so you need to move out," she said, quieting down.

"If you take the kids out of California I'll have you arrested," Richard snarled. "And as far as me moving out, that will never happen. This is my house and I will never move out." He held open the door to his office and motioned for her to leave.

Josie set the table for dinner, putting her plate on one end and Richard's on the other and the kid's plates in the middle, as usual. Before they could sit down to eat, both kids moved their plates as close to Josie as they could. Austen said "Daddy scary" and tried to sit on her lap. She didn't bother to move the plates back to where they belonged.

Richard glowered from his end of the table. The family ate in silence for several minutes. Then Richard abruptly stood up and moved Austen's plate next to his, before roughly pulling the little boy's chair next to him also. Then he shook pepper all over Austen's food.

"Don't like pepper. Don't like pepper, Daddy." Austen started to cry and ran to his mother.

"Thanks for ruining another family meal, Richard. You can eat by yourself from now on." Josie picked up Austen and left the table with Phoebe following close behind.

❦ 4 ❦

After cleaning up the dinner dishes and putting the kids to bed early, Josie went into the office and closed the door. Her voice was low and controlled.

"I understand everything now, Richard. You're an abuser. I don't know what I was thinking. Phoebe's teacher is right - I need to do something about this."

Richard stood up and faced her. "What are you going to do now? File for a divorce?" He said, smirking.

"Yes, Richard, it's over. I want a divorce. I didn't realize what a terrible parent you would turn out to be. You hurt our kids. How dare you."

Josie was surprisingly calm as she heard herself say the word 'divorce.' Richard took a step closer. He got right in her face and smiled menacingly.

"So you mean we get to have a war? We get to have a nuclear war, with lawyers and everything?"

Josie looked at his face and suddenly realized that this was the happiest she'd seen him in years. She glared at him and left the room.

Not wanting to sleep in her bedroom, she went downstairs and made up the bed in the nanny suite they'd set up before the kids were born, but had never used. She climbed between the cold, unfamiliar sheets, and was just drifting off to sleep when she felt both kids and the dog on the bed next to her.

"Mommy, we want to sleep down here with you. We're scared of Daddy," Phoebe said. Austen snuggled next to Josie with his stuffed monkey, while Phoebe covered him with her baby blanket. The dog curled into a ball at the foot of the bed.

"Okay, but just for tonight. It's been a hard day and I'm too tired to put you guys back to bed." Josie lifted her covers over the kids and put her arm around them as they all drifted off to sleep.

The thick forest surrounding Josie was an impenetrable layer of green that reached hundreds of feet into the sky. A thin shaft of sunlight illuminated the path she walked on. The forest was silent, except for the soft sound of her footfalls and the rustling of her skirt. She descended for miles, deep into a valley.

The path ended abruptly and a small pond shimmered before her, perfectly mirroring the vegetation surrounding it. Josie fell to her knees and leaned close to the clear, still water. She scooped her hands and bent down to splash her face, when she suddenly saw the tawny image of a mountain lion staring back at her. Startled, she gasped and turned around.

She scanned the dense brush for the lion and saw nothing. Standing up, she steadied herself against a boulder. She tilted her head back as far as she could, and peered into the canopy high above her. No sign of a mountain lion anywhere. Thirsty from her long trek, she turned and knelt down again to the clear pool of water.

As she leaned in, the mountain lion appeared again. She froze and stared at its shimmering image. The animal stared back with piercing, gold-flecked eyes. She moved her head to one side and the lion's head followed. She moved again, and again the lion followed. The lion mirrored her every move precisely.

She looked down at her hands, her arms, her legs and her body. She felt her face, her long smooth hair, and her soft dress. Everything was just as before. She was still Josie. But when she looked back into the magical reflecting pond, the image of the mountain lion stared back at her. She looked into the lion's eyes for a long moment and he suddenly let out a loud piercing scream. The sound vibrated through her body and she shuddered.

Josie opened her eyes and peered through the darkness of the unfamiliar room. The house was silent. A few seconds passed, and then she noticed Richard standing in the doorway staring at her and the children, the dog at his feet. Startled, she gasped and sat up. She slipped out of bed and approached him. He backed away. She followed him into the dark hall and closed the door behind her.

"What are you doing? Why are you standing there staring at us?"

She whispered sharply. He didn't respond and started towards the stairs. "Richard – there is one more thing I want to say to you." He stopped and faced her.

"I want you to think of me as a mother lion. I will not let you hurt these kids." She stared at him with hatred in her eyes as he retreated up the stairs. Then she returned to the nanny suite and bolted the door behind her.

5

"Mom, I need help. I told Richard I'm going to divorce him and I have to get a restraining order. I'm totally overwhelmed." Josie's mother, Valerie, lived nearby after moving from Montana to be closer to her and the kids. It had been almost a year since Josie's father had died unexpectedly, and Valerie was still adjusting to widowhood.

"Josie, I hate to say this but I saw it coming," Valerie replied. "Before your father died we'd decided that we'd never spend another Thanksgiving at your house, because we couldn't bear to see how Richard yelled at and humiliated the kids. Especially poor little Phoebe. It was just too much for us."

"I know, Mom, I don't know what I was thinking. Anyway, I need help. I'm going to ask Adele to go to court with me, and I was hoping you'd watch Austen. I don't know how long it will take. I can drop him off at your place to make it easier." Josie always hesitated to ask her mother for help, but the situation demanded it.

"Sure, just call me before you get here," Valerie said.

"Thanks, Mom." Josie hung up the phone.

"Hi Adele, it's Josie. I'm sorry to bother you but I need a favor. I have to go to family court, and I was hoping you'd come with me. I need someone to hand court papers to Richard, and I need some moral support because I feel like I'm on the verge of collapse."

Adele was the mother of one of Josie's college friends. During Josie's occasional breaks from her job overseas, she would often stay with Adele and they'd become good friends. Small and compact, with salt and pepper hair and a ready smile, Adele frequently traveled unaccompanied throughout the world. She'd hiked Mount Fuji and explored the ruins of Machu Pichu. At seventy-six, she'd just returned from a solo trip to Mongolia. Adele was one of the most adventuresome and fearless women Josie knew.

"Sure, Josie, I'll help. I've never served papers before, and I am just a little old lady, but it can't be too hard."

"Thanks Adele, I've figured out a way to do it – we'll be waiting next to his car at the BART station and you can just walk over, say his name, hand him the papers and jump back in my car. Then we'll leave."

Josie ended her call and put her key in the front door. She'd just returned from walking Phoebe to school, and heard the house phone ringing as soon as she stepped inside. She hastily pulled Austen from his stroller before sprinting up the stairs and grabbing the phone. The caller I.D. said 'unknown number,' but Josie knew it was CPS. She was expecting their call. "This is Josie," she answered.

"Josephine Bain? We have a report about suspected child abuse, and we need to interview both you and your husband." It was the no-nonsense, authoritarian voice of a middle-aged woman.

"Okay, sure, no problem. I can talk to you pretty much any time."

"We'll see you this morning at eleven. Please arrive early and register. Your social worker is Melinda Grimes."

"Okay, I'll be there." Josie hung up the phone and collapsed into a chair. It was really happening. This wasn't somebody else's life with restraining orders and appointments at social services, this was her life and it was still hard to grasp.

Josie scrolled through her cell phone for the number of her therapist in Berkeley. She hadn't seen her for over two years, but she really needed to talk to someone now. She dialed the number. "Hello, this is Josie Bain. You treated me a while back and I was wondering if you were available." She was in the middle of leaving a message when the therapist came on the line.

"Josie, it's been a while. What can I do for you?"

"Hi, Dianne, I'm having some problems and I'd just really like to come in and talk – like today if possible."

"Can you come now? I have a cancelation this morning."

"Yes, I'll take it," Josie said. "I have to drop my son off first and I'll get there as soon as I can."

She had barely taken a seat on the worn leather sofa in the therapist's office when the story spilled out of her: Richard yelling, Phoebe crying, the numerous confrontations, the conversation with the teacher and the appointment at CPS. After several minutes, Josie finally stopped talking and looked at the therapist.

Dianne Harper, a manicured and stylish woman in her late forties, with short gray hair and a calm soothing manner, cleared her throat and spoke softly.

"Josie, I agree with Phoebe's teacher. Richard needs to move out. In fact, I'm also a mandated reporter and I will be calling CPS myself after this session is over."

"What? But I needed you to help me navigate through this. That's why I came here. I don't need anyone else turning us in. It's just that it's all happening so fast. I don't have a plan. I have nothing to fall back on. Richard said he's going to go nuclear on me – with lawyers and everything. This can't be happening. I can't do this," Josie pleaded.

"I'm sorry," Dianne replied. "I know this is hard, but you don't have time to think it over. You're seeing the social worker today and she'll tell you the same thing: Richard has to move out."

"Yes, I know – but I feel like someone just picked up my entire world, held it upside down and shook it as hard as they could, then set it back down and somehow I'm supposed to just get back on my feet and pretend everything's fine and take care of business. I need time to process everything. I'm just trying to get my bearings here." Josie slapped the couch with her hand.

The therapist started to recommend a book when Josie noticed the time. "Actually, I have to go now. I'm sorry. I only have twenty-five minutes to get to CPS on time."

She left the therapist's office and sped toward the freeway. Driving east through the tunnel, the familiar suburbs flew past her speeding car. Enveloped in her thoughts, Josie nearly missed the turnoff for the CPS office. She parked in front of the bland government building and went in.

The ugly, utilitarian office furniture and the bare tile floors gave it an aura of the Soviet Union circa 1970. Hugging her purse and tapping her foot nervously, she checked in and sat down on a cracked vinyl chair. Noticing what appeared to be one-way mirrors lining the back wall, Josie assumed she was being observed by some anonymous social worker. She sat up straight and folded her hands on her lap. She couldn't help but feel that the people in this office regarded her with disdain. To them she was just another low-life parent who'd been reported for child abuse.

A heavy-set woman in her fifties called Josie's name and led her to a small windowless room. Melinda Grimes sat down at her desk and opened the folder in front of her. Josie sat down opposite her.

"I spoke to your daughter yesterday, Mrs. Bain." Ms. Grimes began. "She's a very smart girl. We've opened an investigation, and both you and your husband will be interviewed."

"So," she continued. "Have you ever seen your husband hit Phoebe or her brother? Have you ever noticed any marks on them that could have come from your husband?"

Josie told the social worker everything she could remember – the sound of Phoebe's head getting knocked against the wall, the bruise on Austen's face, the kid's crying, Richard yelling, Phoebe constantly saying 'I hate Daddy'- everything she could think of. Ms. Grimes took notes the whole time.

When Josie stopped talking, the social worker put her pen down and leaned forward at her desk. "Mrs. Bain." She paused and looked Josie in the eye. "You must protect your children. If you fail to protect them we will remove them from the home and place them in foster care. Furthermore, you and the children can no longer live with your husband. I don't know what your relationship with him is like but you can still see him – you can go on dates with him if you want – but you can't live in the same house with him and the children. Do you understand?" Her tone was harsh, and Josie felt like a criminal.

"Yes, Ms. Grimes. I understand completely. I am talking to Richard now about him moving out. I'm taking care of it." Josie was contrite.

"It needs to happen quickly, Mrs. Bain. You will be considered just as guilty as he is if this situation continues. It is called 'failure to protect' and it is a serious charge," she added. "You may go now."

6

Richard went straight into his office when he got home that evening. His anger radiated throughout the house, and tension filled the air. Josie told the children to play in their rooms. She entered the office and Richard glowered at her from behind his desk. She got right to the point.

"It's over, Richard. You need to leave. This is your last warning. I was interviewed by CPS today, and they said I would be in trouble if the children and I continued to live with you. I refuse to get in trouble for something I didn't do. You broke our marriage. You broke our family. You anger has destroyed everything we've worked so hard for."

Richard was silent. He fists were clenched, his jaw was tight and his mouth was twisted into a snarl. "I will not leave," he growled. "This is my house. If you want to leave, feel free, but you're not taking the kids. I will not discuss this further."

"Richard, you have to leave. If you don't leave tonight I will get a court order tomorrow and I will make you leave. I have no other choice."

He sprang to his feet. "Get out of my office. I'm done talking about this!"

The next day Josie picked up Adele and drove to the courthouse. There were men and women in business suits, young families with children, people of every ethnicity and from every walk of life crowded into the room. The full cross section of Bay Area demographics was funneled into one building, into family court.

"No matter your background, if your family falls apart the pieces will end up here," Adele whispered to Josie as they stood in line. Adele's own marriage had been difficult, but she was from a different era and she'd stuck it out until her husband passed away.

In one corner of the room a young woman cowered in fear, while two small children clung tightly to her legs. A young man screamed at her from a few feet away. He looked as if he was about to lunge at her, and he probably would have, were it not for the two steely-eyed bailiffs with guns in their holsters flanking him on both sides. The woman looked down, clearly scared and humiliated. Josie looked over at Adele and bit her lip. It was hard for her to believe that she was standing in line with such desperate people, and was asking for the same protection they were seeking.

After a two hour wait, the clerk called her name and Josie went to the window. The clerk slipped Josie's paperwork through the small opening and robotically recited the procedure for serving the papers, never bothering to look up.

"Are you sure you really need this, Josie?" Adele asked as they left the building. "It's not like Richard is one of those screaming maniacs like that young man we saw." Adele had never seen Richard yell at or hurt the children, and even though she found him cold and unlikeable, it was hard for her to believe he was in the same category as such an obviously violent man as they'd just witnessed.

"No one ever sees him hit the children, Adele. I don't even see him do it. He's a different kind of abuser. He's a clever abuser. He knows better than to do anything physical when there are witnesses. He will berate and yell at the kids in front of me, but he pulls his punches when I'm in the room," Josie said.

"Well, let's get this over with then. Don't forget, I'm just a little old lady and I don't want any trouble."

"There won't be any trouble, Adele," Josie assured her. "You said yourself he's not that kind of guy – he would never act out in public, especially against a little old lady."

Adele and Josie arrived at the BART lot and headed straight for Richard's usual parking spot. It was about twenty minutes before his train was due to arrive. His car wasn't there.

"Oh my God," said Josie. "His car is always here and he never goes home early."

"Maybe this time he did, Josie." Adele was nervous. "Listen, I'm okay with surprising him at a BART lot, handing him some papers and leaving, but I don't feel comfortable confronting him at his own home, which is where he probably is."

"I know Adele, I'm not comfortable with that either. In fact, I'm not comfortable with the whole thing. I mean two days ago my life consisted of making meals and taking care of kids and now I'm about to serve my husband a restraining order. Listen, I'll drop you back at your house and rethink this. Maybe I can talk him into leaving. That would be best for everyone."

"Good thinking," Adele agreed.

Josie drove Adele home and picked up the kids from her mother's house. She headed back to her house, full of trepidation. She had the restraining order in her purse, and she was never good at lying. If Richard had gone home early he'd want to know where she was.

When she pulled around the corner, she saw that his car wasn't there and the house was dark.

After she'd tucked the kids into bed that evening, she locked all the doors and checked all the windows. She sat up late reading, unable to sleep. Plan 'A' hadn't worked, and she had to think of a plan 'B.' Adele was right – she was a little old lady and Josie was wrong to get her involved in this. The clerk at the courthouse had said something about notifying the local police that she had a restraining order against her husband. Josie was mulling over whether to call them.

Suddenly she heard something. Her dog jumped off the bed and cocked his head to listen, his tail wagging slightly. When he didn't bark, Josie immediately knew that it was Richard trying to sneak into the house. It was almost midnight. She scrambled off the bed and grabbed the phone. Her heart was pounding. She'd given him an ultimatum and he'd ignored her. He must know that she had a restraining order against him.

She quickly turned the lock on the inside of her bedroom door and put on her robe. Then she quietly opened the French doors leading out to the garden. Running barefoot over the deck, and down the side stairs, she saw Richard's car parked in the driveway, close to the house. It was empty.

It's now or never, Josie thought. Breathing heavily, and hearing her heart pounding in her throat, she dialed the police.

"Hello, I'm Josephine Bain. I live at one thirty-five Patricia Court and my husband just snuck into the house. I have a restraining order against him. I'm alone and my kids are inside sleeping. I need help."

"Is there a gun?" The dispatcher asked. "Are there any weapons? Is he dangerous? Are you in a safe place?"

"No, no guns. I'm standing outside on the driveway. I snuck out the back door when I heard him come in. I don't think he'd try to hurt a police officer. I think he knows I have a restraining order, but I haven't served it to him yet. We couldn't find him."

"Okay. Do you have the restraining order with you?"

"No, but it's in my purse in my bedroom. I locked the bedroom door before I left. I can probably sneak back in and get it." Josie's emotional floodgates were now flung open wide, and fear was gushing out.

"No, that isn't necessary. Wait right where you are. An officer will arrive shortly. He will go back inside with you, and you can give it to him then. He will serve your husband with the order."

"Thank you so much," Josie gushed, grateful and relieved that she didn't have to sneak back in there alone.

Two tall, burly officers arrived a few minutes later and parked their cars at the bottom of the driveway. Josie led them through the back door and handed the restraining order to one of them. She unlocked her bedroom door and peeked into the hallway. Seeing the light from Richard's office, she pointed the men in that direction.

As the policemen went down the dark hallway, Phoebe tiptoed out of her bedroom from the other direction, carrying Austen. "Mommy, I couldn't sleep. I heard something and I didn't know where you were," the little girl whispered.

Josie shushed her daughter and motioned the children into her bedroom. She closed the door and the three of them sat on the bed together, holding each other in a group hug.

"It's okay sweetie. Daddy will be leaving soon. The police officers will tell him to move out. Everything will be okay. Nobody is going to get hurt." Josie spoke calmly, trying to reassure herself, as much as the children.

She listened intently, thinking there might be a commotion. Richard never hesitated to raise his voice to her and the children, and she could imagine his anger and shock when he looked up and saw two police officers enter his office late at night. Instead, she heard nothing. It was eerily quiet.

Finally, there were muffled voices and the sound of the front door closing. Then the officers entered her bedroom again.

"We served the restraining order ma'am. Your husband would like some of his clothing before he leaves," one officer told her.

"Okay, no problem. I have a duffle already packed." Josie reached into Richard's closet and handed the officer a large bag. "Thank you again for helping me. You don't know how grateful I am."

Austen looked up in awe at the officers, mesmerized by their gold badges and their guns.

"If you have anyone that can come here and stay with you we recommend it, at least for tonight," one of the officers said, as his partner gave both kids shiny gold police badge stickers and patted Austen's head.

"Cute kids," one of them remarked, as they left out the back door.

Austen and Phoebe jumped on Josie's bed laughing. They jumped off again and chased each other around the house, shrieking with joy.

"It's a party, Mommy. We're having a party!" Phoebe said brightly, jumping back on Josie's bed, doing summersaults and tumbling around with her brother.

"It's late, Phoebe. You should both be in bed. There's school tomorrow." Josie scolded the children half-heartedly as it dawned on her that this was the happiest she'd ever seen them. In one remarkable moment, their tears had dried up and the smiles came out. It was a momentous occasion in Josie's life. Phoebe was right - it was time for a party.

Rummaging around in the kitchen cupboards, she found a small, exquisitely decorated box that was tied with a blue satin ribbon. Inside were six perfect handmade chocolate truffles that she'd purchased on a whim a few weeks earlier.

"I was saving these for some reason and now I know why – it's for our special party!" Josie settled onto the couch, the children piling on her lap. "Today is our own personal independence day, children – the sixth of December. We need to celebrate. You can each have two." Josie had barely cracked open the lid, when two small hands started grabbing chocolates. The children laughed and stuffed the candy into their mouths.

∽ 7 ∾

For the first few days after Richard left, Josie luxuriated in the peace and quiet that had descended on her home. There was no more anger. No more yelling. No more crying. She didn't know what to expect next, but she knew one thing for sure: she'd never again share a roof with the 'madman' she'd married and for that she was thankful.

She sipped her tea and gazed out the living room window at the sweeping, pastoral view of her leafy suburban neighborhood. As soon as she'd seen the view, Josie had known this was the right house for them. She and Richard both had good jobs – she was an engineer and he was in IT. She also had income from property she'd purchased while she was in her twenties, before her marriage. She'd worked overseas her first few years out of college, and with a substantial paycheck and company-paid accommodations, she was able to purchase three apartment houses back in her hometown in Montana.

With their combined incomes, and Josie's rental income they could easily afford to move to this up-market neighborhood, which had the best schools in the Bay Area.

The phone rang. "Hi, Josie, this is Andrew. Richard asked Phil and me to stop by the house and get more of his things. He wants the rest of his clothes and some of his tools. Does tomorrow morning work for you?" Andrew was one of Richard's cousins, and a favorite of both Phoebe and Austen.

"Yes Andrew, no problem. The kids will be happy to see you again." Christmas was approaching, and Josie was sad that the kids wouldn't be spending it with the rest of Richard's family as they usually did. She knew that his family would close ranks around him. Of course, they only knew what he chose to tell them. Whenever they visited his family, Richard was on his good behavior. They never saw him mistreat the children, and Josie assumed they were probably stunned at the turn of events.

The following morning, Andrew swept both kids up into his arms as he stepped into the house. Richard's old family friend, Phil, stood in the doorway behind Andrew loaded down with Christmas presents. Phoebe and Austen were thrilled.

"Okay kids, let them in the door and help Phil put the presents under the tree." Josie instructed the children as the men stepped into the house.

"Uh, right, could you show me where Richard keeps his things?" Andrew addressed Josie coldly and avoided looking at her.

"Yes – most of his stuff is in the bedroom down the hall, and his tools are downstairs in the garage."

The older man, Phil, carried two large shopping bags brimming with Christmas gifts into the living room. He greeted Josie and clasped her hand warmly. Short and wiry, with a full head of white hair and watery blue eyes, Phil had originally been a good friend of Richard's father.

"Hello, Josie! It's so good to see you again!" Phil boomed, smiling broadly. The kids started putting the presents under the tree, while Phil good naturedly chatted with their mother. He asked about the remodeling that Richard had done on the house since he'd last visited years earlier and about Josie's plans for the holidays. Relieved that at least Phil was being friendly, Josie relaxed and showed him around.

While she was downstairs showing Phil the nanny suite that she and Richard had worked on, Andrew went into the office and deftly looked through the couple's filing cabinet. He dug in his pocket for the list of files that Richard had given him, quietly lifting each of them out of the cabinet and setting them aside. Then he removed a wrapped bundle from his duffle bag and set it on the floor. He could hear Phil talking to Josie in a loud voice, peppering her with questions about the house.

Working quickly, he disconnected the computer's processing unit and replaced it with the one that he'd brought with him. The two devices looked almost identical and he figured Josie would never notice. Then he wrapped up the files, along with the CPU, and stuffed them into the duffle bag. He gently pushed the file cabinet drawer closed, and went into the master bedroom. He flung open Richard's closet door and grabbed a handful of the remaining shirts and ties and threw those into the duffle before zipping it closed.

Finished with his task, Andrew called down the stairs to his accomplice. "Okay – I think we're good – we need to get going," he said.

"Sounds good," Phil yelled back and the two men walked out the front door. Phil shook Josie's hand again as he left, and she watched from the porch as Andrew put the duffle bag into the back of his car. Josie and the kids waved goodbye as they drove off.

"What a mess," Josie sighed, picking hangers and shirts up from the bedroom floor and putting them back in the closet. She opened the other side of the closet and saw that the rest of Richard's trousers and jackets were untouched. She opened one of his dresser drawers and everything was exactly as she'd left it.

"So he basically has the things I packed for him plus a few more shirts and ties," she mused out loud.

"Mommy, is something wrong?" Phoebe stood looking at her mother. Without waiting for an answer she blurted out, "Andrew brought us Christmas presents! Can we each open one now?"

"No sweetie, not now. Just arrange them under the tree. Austen can help you. I just have a strange feeling. It was strange seeing Phil again. I haven't seen him in years – and Andrew was acting odd. He wouldn't look me in the eye."

Josie went into the office and turned on the computer. While it was booting up, she grabbed the phone and went to check on the kids. Austen was shaking one of the presents, and Phoebe was carefully lifting the taped edge of the Christmas wrapping on another one.

"Just put the presents under the tree, no cheating you guys." She dialed the phone and called her mother.

"Phil and Andrew were here today. They came over to get some of Richard's stuff and brought presents for the kids." Valerie was in the kitchen of her condo in Oakmoor, a large retirement village about five miles away from Josie.

"What did they say?"

"Not much. Andrew had a duffle bag but he didn't really take that much from Richard's' closet, and he never went in the garage to get the tools he said Richard wanted. I haven't seen Phil in years – not since his manslaughter trial – do you remember, Mom? Three of his tenants died because of some shoddy work at one of the buildings he owns in the city, and it turned out there were no inspections or permits, and it was basically an accident waiting to happen. I have to say, it was strange seeing him again after all these years. He totally schmoozed me, and acted as if nothing was wrong as far as Richard and me."

"Of course I remember Phil. We met him at your wedding. He sat at our table – a real schmoozer, that guy. I remember his case too – you told me all about it." Valerie paused and poured herself a cup of coffee. "I never said anything while you and Richard were together, but there are a lot of things I've been wondering about over the years. Like, why this guy Phil turned out to be a notorious building code scofflaw, and yet he was best friends with Richard's father – who was the chief building code enforcement officer for the city?" Valerie sat down and muted the TV so she could talk to her daughter. She was a confirmed cynic and was often troubled by Josie's naiveté.

"Yeah, you're right, Mom. I never really thought about that before. Now that I think about it, Phil being good friends with Richard's father is sort of like a notorious criminal being good friends with the chief of police. It doesn't make sense. They should have been enemies. But instead, here we are, several years after Richard's father passed away and Phil is in my house helping Richard." Josie sat on the couch and watched as the children rearranged the ornaments on the Christmas tree.

"I always thought it was suspicious. Your in-laws were quick to tell you that Richard's father had a sixth-grade education, and yet had amassed a fortune in Bay Area real estate on a city bureaucrat's salary. Meanwhile, your father and his friends were all highly educated men and none of them attained anywhere near the wealth that Richard's father managed to do. Of course, university professors seldom get rich, especially in Montana, but still, I think there's a lot more to the story of the Bain family fortune than we know." Valerie glanced at her watch. "Listen, Josie, I'm playing bridge in half an hour, do you need anything?"

"I was getting to that, Mom. I received a notice to appear in court next week and I'm nervous. I have to go before the judge about the restraining order." Austen had climbed into Josie's lap holding one of the presents.

"Well, let me know if you need help. I have a little money and I can help if you need it."

"Thanks, Mom, that makes me feel better. Richard has always been pretty cheap, so I can't really see him spending a bunch of money on lawyers. On the other hand, he seemed so gleeful when I told him I was divorcing him and he said something like 'oh boy we get to have a war with lawyers and everything.' I can only assume that Phil is advising him about this situation and probably told him to get lawyered up. Richard said himself that if it wasn't for his high-dollar attorneys, Phil would be rotting in jail right now on that manslaughter charge." Josie said goodbye and hung up the phone.

❦ 8 ❦

Digging through the back of her closet, Josie found the light gray business suit she used to wear to important work meetings. She ironed the suit along with a plain white dress shirt. Her hair was pulled back in a neat bun, and her face was lightly made up. She found some dark leggings and the black pumps she hadn't worn in years. The hearing wasn't until one o'clock, but she planned to head over to her mother's place early to drop off Austen and hang out for a while.

She got pregnant with Austen at the age of thirty-six and was sick from the beginning. Her poor health had caught her by surprise because she'd breezed through her first pregnancy and barely even had morning sickness. She was almost five years older the second time around, but was fit and active. She prided herself on her good health and had never had anything more serious than an occasional migraine. After a series of emergency visits to the doctor with early bleeding, she was put on bed rest for the last five months of the pregnancy.

Josie and Richard went together to a follow-up appointment after she'd visited the emergency room. When the doctor prescribed bed rest for the remainder of the pregnancy, Richard became glum. They drove home in silence and as he pulled the car into the garage he exploded. "How is this supposed to work?" He raged. "You don't have that much sick leave!" He got out, slamming the car door behind him. Josie got out on her side.

"Richard, calm down. We'll be fine. We have the income from my properties and I have about three weeks of sick leave. We'll just have to be careful. Anyway, it is what it is – we have to make it work." Josie tried to reassure him.

"Then, when the bed rest is over you'll be on pregnancy leave for another three months!" Richard shook his head.

"Really, Richard – is that all you care about? Is money the only thing you care about? What about me? What about the baby? Sometimes I wonder why you even wanted to get married and have kids. My dad always told me that there are no guarantees in life. We aren't guaranteed to have an easy pregnancy and we aren't guaranteed to always have two incomes. We'll get through this because that's what we do – we persevere." Josie went upstairs while Richard got back in the car and drove away.

She sat down on the couch and called her boss. They'd worked together for years and had the same alma mater. Initially he'd been reluctant to hire a woman engineer, but Josie had turned out to be one of his best employees.

"Hi Mark, I have bad news. The doctor ordered bed rest. You're going to have to give my project to someone else. I don't know exactly how long. I have twenty-three weeks to go, and then another twelve weeks after the baby comes. About eight months total. I'll send the note from my doctor."

Mark paused and took in the news. It wasn't unexpected. Josie had gone home sick several times in the last month. She was having a difficult pregnancy and was still trying to do it all. "It's alright, Josie. Just take care of yourself. We'll figure it out."

"Thanks Mark. I'm lucky to have you for a boss. Also, I have a favor to ask you."

"Sure, what is it?"

"I know you're looking for a new IT guy and I was really hoping you'd consider Richard. He's seriously under-utilized in his current position. I know you'd be happy with his work. Anyway, please give it some thought." If she could help Richard get a higher paying job, Josie assumed it would ease his worries about money.

Josie was under doctor's orders to restrict her movements – only walking short distances and no lifting. Her mother did the grocery shopping and helped around the house when she had time. Josie made a list of things for Richard to take care of – mostly easy things like walking down their steep driveway to get the mail, something she'd always done in the past. Little did she know that such a small thing would have such grave repercussions for her future.

9

After being induced when she hit the thirty-eight week mark, Josie gave birth to a perfect ten-pound baby boy with a full head of dark curly hair and bright blue eyes. Richard sat quietly in the corner of the hospital room and was subdued when the time came to hold his son.

Later, when he brought Phoebe to the hospital to visit, he was irritable. Phoebe announced brightly that she was going to be Austen's 'other mother' and Richard snapped at her to shut up. Josie had adapted to Richard's increasingly angry demeanor by trying to ignore it. She sensed that he was trying to provoke a fight and Josie went to great lengths to avoid confrontations. He was forty-seven when Austen was born and she assumed it was some sort of mid-life crisis that would pass in time. She pushed his anger away and tiptoed around it as best she could.

One of Josie's first calls when she returned home from the hospital was to her boss, Mark. She hadn't spoken to him for months and had never thanked him for bringing Richard into the company, at a substantial increase in salary over his last job. She knew Richard was hired on his merits, but she also knew her boss considered him in the first place because of her.

"Congratulations on your son, Josie. And by the way, Richard is working out well. He came up to speed quickly. He's quiet but he takes care of business. To tell you the truth I only considered him as a favor to you but he's turned out to be a good hire." As he spoke, Mark pulled Josie's personnel file and glanced through it.

"Also, when you have time, there's something you need to look into – no rush – I know you're busy. There's some kind of problem with your state engineering license. We received a letter from the state about three weeks ago. I didn't want to bother you with it at the time. Apparently your license didn't renew. It must be some sort of mix-up. You'll need to take care of that before you can come back to work."

"Thanks Mark. I'll look into it right away." Josie hung up the phone, suddenly feeling a pit in her stomach.

She walked into the kitchen and found Richard popping open a beer. "Richard, did you see my license renewal? It must have come in the mail a few weeks ago. Somehow I didn't get it. It must have come when I was on bed rest. I know if I'd been at work Mark would have flagged it because he's always on top of that stuff, but I was at home and I never saw the notice. Do you know anything about it?" Josie was more perplexed than accusatory.

"Your license is your responsibility," Richard stated flatly before leaving the room and turning on the TV.

"Did you see the renewal notice or not? They always send a notice to my house. You were bringing the mail the last few months – what happened to it?" Josie followed him, and began to raise her voice. Richard turned the volume up and ignored her.

When she called the state licensing office the next day she assumed she'd probably be fined for late renewal and that would be that. No biggie.

"You'll have to retake the license exam Mrs. Bain," the clerk told her. Josie was flabbergasted.

"That's ridiculous! Just because I was a few weeks late? Don't I get a grace period? Do you have any idea what that exam consists of? It's an all-day written exam, followed by an oral exam in front of a panel of experts. I can't just retake that exam! It took me months of studying to pass it in the first place – and that was before I was married and had kids! I have a newborn baby – how in the world am I supposed to study for a grueling two day exam?" Josie was yelling into the phone.

"Mrs. Bain you need to calm down. I'm sorry. Your renewal grace period expired last month. You need to retake the exam." Josie hung up the phone. She put her hands to her face. Her head was throbbing from a migraine, and Austen was crying in the next room. She took stock of her life: a five year old, a new baby, a cold and distant husband, and no livelihood. With no license she couldn't go back to her old job. She was devastated.

Josie laid the gray suit on the bed and looked it over again as she thought about the last few years. She was still very bitter about her license. Months after confronting Richard about it, she was rummaging around in his office and found the renewal notice under a pile of papers. Richard denied knowing anything about it. She never retook the exam. She never had time. Her rental property was bringing in good money and Richard had a much better job – thanks in part to her. They were still doing fine financially, as far as Josie was concerned.

It occurred to her on many occasions that she'd helped his career, while he had sabotaged hers, perhaps deliberately. 'I wouldn't doubt it,' her mother had said to her when they talked about it once 'that's what men do dear.'

Josie was pleased that the suit still fit. She picked up Austen and grabbed the diaper bag before heading over to her mother's house. After pulling out of the garage, she parked at the bottom of the driveway and got out to grab the mail.

She got back in the car and tossed the mail on the seat next to her. Then she noticed an official looking envelope and picked it up. It was from the Diablo Valley Law Firm and was addressed to her. She tore it open. Inside was a legal document several pages long. She flipped through it and saw a statement signed by Phil, Richard's old family friend.

He'd signed an affidavit swearing that Josie had confided in him that she'd actually kicked Richard out of the house because she had another man lined up and that she had fabricated the abuse charges against Richard in order to get custody of the kids.

"Huh?" Josie said out loud, incredulous. In the second paragraph he claimed that Austen had rushed up to him when he'd brought over the Christmas presents and said 'are you my new daddy? Are you my new daddy? Mommy says I have a new daddy!'

"Oh my God! This is unbelievable!" She shrieked and threw the papers down. Austen started to cry in the back seat. She started the car and drove to Oakmoor.

⌒ 10 ⌒

Josie set Austen down in the living room of her mother's small condo before sitting down at the kitchen table, disgusted. "So, there's all of fifty-three dollars in our checking account today. I guess Richard beat me to it. How am I supposed to pay the mortgage and utilities?" Josie sighed.

"I've heard that's the first thing they do – clear out the bank account. Is there a savings account – any other money you can get your hands on?" Valerie asked.

"Not really – we just keep a nominal amount in our savings. Most of our savings is in the brokerage account and I need both signatures to get that. So, I guess, at least he can't get it either." Josie stood up and started to pace. "And there's another thing – I couldn't get the computer to boot up. Just when I really need it, the stupid computer quits working." Josie glanced over at Austen who was absorbed in his drawing.

"Well, I wouldn't be so sure he can't get the brokerage money since he's friends with the broker, Josie. Anyway, I have a little money I can give you – it isn't much but it's all I can afford." Valerie's only income was from her social security and a small pension Josie's father had left her.

"Richard is going to have to at least pay the mortgage or give you money for that. You're going to need a lawyer, Josie – I'll give you some money to get you started with that."

"Thanks Mom, but I don't need an attorney. There's free legal assistance at the courthouse. I was planning to go before the hearing and sign up for the free help. We have so much equity in the house, I can't believe Richard would do anything stupid like not pay the mortgage or at least give me money to pay it. Oh, I almost forgot – this was in the mailbox when I left." Josie handed Phil's affidavit to her mother.

"Wow, Josie. So Richard already has an attorney. And this is incredible. Did this really happen? Did Austen really say that to Phil?" Valerie looked up from reading the court filing.

"No, of course not, Mother. It's all a lie. The whole thing is completely made up. But since he was there with Andrew they can probably say anything they want. It's two against one. I was stupid to even let them in the house." Josie sat down and sipped her coffee.

"Are you nervous about the hearing this afternoon?" Valerie asked.

"Yes, of course. The whole thing freaks me out. Being at the courthouse that day with Adele was a total nightmare. Some guy was screaming at this woman and her kids were plastered to her legs, sobbing. There were two bailiffs standing there watching with their hands on their holsters. This whole thing is a nightmare. I keep hoping I'll wake up and it will all go away." Josie stood up and put her purse over her shoulder. She bent down and kissed Austen and left.

At the courthouse, a slender, grim-faced woman with closely cropped hair called Josie's number and motioned her over to her desk. "What can I do for you?" She said briskly.

"I have a hearing today about a restraining order." Josie tried to be calm and collected. "My husband was abusive to our children, and we are being investigated by CPS. He took all the money out of the checking account and I can't pay any of the bills. Honestly, I don't know what to do and I need help. I need legal help." The words poured out of her as Josie dug through her bag for a pen and paper.

The woman had a detached look on her face as she took in Josie's neatly pressed business suit and expensive shoes. "I'm sorry. I can't help you. You have major child support and property issues. You need a lawyer," she said bluntly.

"I can't get a lawyer. I don't think you heard me. I can't even pay the mortgage. He took all the money. I've been waiting here for over an hour and I need help." Josie was incredulous.

"Listen, this service is for very basic family law filings. It is not for people with major support issues such as you. I can get you a list of family law attorneys in our jurisdiction if you need it." The woman looked blankly at Josie and shrugged.

Josie walked away as the woman called another number. She went outside and dialed her mother. "They refused to help me. I waited over an hour and all she said was 'get a lawyer.' Like, tell me something I don't already know. If I had the money I would get a lawyer and I wouldn't have bothered with her - duh!"

"Okay, Josie, when you get back today I'll take some money out of my savings for a retainer. Hopefully this case can be settled quickly." Valerie hung up and sighed heavily as she cut up an apple for her grandson.

Josie stood alone at the end of the corridor and watched as small groups of two and three people filed into the courtroom. Suddenly, Richard and Phil come around the corner, accompanied by large balding man who looked like a stuffed sausage in his three piece suit.

That must be the lawyer, Josie thought. The men were talking and didn't notice Josie watching them from a few yards away.

She went in and found a seat in the back corner of the gallery, opposite Richard and his entourage. When the bailiff called their names, Richard followed his attorney through a small swinging gate and sat down at a table in front of the judge. Josie stood up and nervously straightened her skirt. She passed through the gate and sat down at the opposite table. It was the first time she'd ever been in court. She'd never had time to watch much TV and wasn't even familiar with courtroom dramas.

The bailiff told Richard and Josie to stand and hold up their hands as they swore to tell the whole truth and nothing but the truth. They sat down and the judge motioned for Richard's attorney to speak.

"Your Honor, I am Adam Wiener, attorney for Richard Bain. We are here to dispute the claims Mrs. Bain made on her restraining order. In fact, Your Honor, my client is a loving father and has never hurt his children in any way. It is my understanding that Mrs. Bain is being treated for emotional problems and she is now trying to perform a complete parentectomy on my client. We ask that you lift the restraining order and restore Mr. Bain's full and unrestricted access to his children." Richard sniffled loudly and wiped away tears as his attorney made the presentation. The attorney pronounced the word 'parentectomy' with a dramatic flourish and turned to scowl at Josie as he said it.

Josie fiddled with the pen and notebook she'd placed on the table in front of her. She suddenly looked up and realized the judge was talking to her. "Mrs. Bain, your husband denies any wrongdoing and wants the restraining order lifted. Do you have anything to say?" The judge leaned forward in his chair and waited for a response.

"Your Honor," Josie cleared her throat. "I'm nervous. I've never been in a courtroom before. Everything I wrote on the restraining order is the truth, Your Honor. My husband repeatedly and consistently hurt our children. We are being investigated by CPS. I ask that you keep the order in place." Josie's heart was pounding in her ears.

"Since there seems to be some complexity in this matter, I am going to have to refer it to a custody evaluator," the judge replied. "Each party will need approximately ten thousand dollars to pay for an evaluation," he said.

"Your Honor, I don't have any money. My husband withdrew all the money from our accounts. I was told I would lose my children if I didn't protect them from my husband. I can't afford to pay for a private evaluator." Josie almost fell out of her chair when she heard the judge say the words 'ten thousand dollars.'

"I'm going keep the restraining order in effect until the next hearing date and I order the parties retain a custody evaluator." The judge banged his gavel and Richard's attorney smirked at Josie as they filed past her. Richard sniffled loudly and wiped away tears as he followed Phil and his attorney out of the courtroom.

❧ 11 ❧

"It was unbelievable, Alice. I should have brought a barf bag to court." Josie called her old friend in Montana and talked animatedly into her cell as she walked the several blocks back to her car. "He was crying and sniffling and wiping away tears, really putting on a show. There were totally fake crocodile tears running down his face. And his lawyer is almost as wide as he is tall with the most God-awful comb-over. Oh, and Phil was there, too – watching from the peanut gallery - sneering and smirking at me the whole time. Walking out of the courtroom they looked like the gruesome threesome." Josie fumbled in her purse for the car keys as she hurried down the street.

"Phil even filled out a completely false affidavit claiming that I'd told him that I threw Richard out of the house in order to have some new guy move in and that I made up all the stuff about the child abuse. Honestly, I still can't believe it, Alice. I remember Richard told me that Phil's father was a judge – so I guess he knows how the system really works." Josie was energized and animated as she spoke. The air was crisp and the streets still had Christmas decorations up. She got in the car and threw her purse on the passenger seat.

"So he's all lawyered up already," Alice observed. "I wouldn't be surprised if he had an attorney all along, Josie. He was planning this. He had no intention of staying in the marriage. He was always so quiet – right from the beginning. He was calculated and cold blooded. Remember that time he deliberately gave me the wrong directions to your house because he didn't want you to have a friend visit? I was driving around lost in the middle of the night and you finally realized it and came and got me? I had a feeling he was an abuser."

Alice talked loudly into her phone as she hiked along the trail near her Montana house. A light snow was falling. She stopped briefly and whistled for her dogs. "Anyway, as I was saying. It sounds like this lawyer is a real piece of work. You do know that divorce attorneys are the lowest of the low on the legal hierarchy? They're the bottom feeders."

Alice's long time boyfriend, Tim, was an attorney specializing in tribal law in Montana. He mostly handled environmental issues affecting some of the reservations in the state. "Much as I hate to see you spend money on one of those guys, you're going to need an attorney. I'll talk to Tim and see if he knows anyone out there." Alice called the dogs again.

"That's okay, Alice. I have a couple of referrals already. The big problem is money. Richard cleared out the checking account." Josie started the car and warmed up the engine.

"Well, I can probably help a little. I'm sure some other friends will help out too," Alice offered.

"Thanks, Alice. My mother is going to take some money out of her savings and get me started with a retainer. The judge said I was going to need ten thousand dollars for a custody evaluator. How are people supposed to be able to do this stuff? Anyway, I have to go now. My mom has Austen and I've got to get back and start figuring out what to do." Josie hung up the phone and drove back to Oakmoor.

⚭ 12 ⚭

The weekend she'd met Richard, over a decade earlier, Josie had gone on what turned out to be her only bicycle club outing. Standing on her bike pedals and pumping as hard as she could, Josie laboriously climbed the long steep hill on the two-lane highway in the Napa wine region. As slow as she was at climbing, she was even worse at the downhill, riding her brakes the entire way.

"I rode a bike all over New Zealand last year but I basically went at my own pace," she told her roommate, Chris, who was riding beside her.

"How in the hell are we supposed to be meeting guys when they're all three miles ahead of us?" Chris said, as rivulets of sweat meandered down the side of her face.

"We're stopping for lunch at the next vineyard. At least the ratios are in our favor. There are about three dozen guys and maybe four women," Josie replied, trying to look on the bright side.

"That's only because most women aren't stupid enough to spend their day off in skin tight black spandex with sweat pouring into their eyes and getting crotch rot on some rock hard bike seat under the blazing hot sun," Chris said. "Whose idea was this anyway?"

"It was your idea," Josie said. "It was all your idea, Chris. Let's join a single's cycling club! We'll meet tons of single guys! What could possibly go wrong? Hey look – here's our turnoff."

The women pulled onto a long tree-lined driveway that wound its way past manicured rows of Cabernet vines. It was the sort of picturesque landscape that tourists come from all over the world to see but the only thing Josie could think about was going home and taking a shower.

Coming around a bend, they saw a couple dozen expensive road bikes leaning against picnic tables and shade trees. The other riders in their group were all sitting down drinking, eating and relaxing.

"Nothing like coming in DFL," Josie said as she clumsily dropped her bike on its side and pulled off her helmet.

"DFL? What's that?" Chris asked, working her fingers through her matted, sweat-soaked hair.

"Dead fucking last," Josie replied, trying to pull her underwear out of her crotch without anyone noticing.

"It's not a race girlfriend. Remember, this is about meeting men," Chris reminded her.

The two friends walked stiffly over to one of the tables, where a tall good-looking man in his late thirties or early forties casually pulled out a plastic chair and motioned for them to sit. "I'm Bruce," he introduced himself. "This is Richard."

Square-jawed, with green eyes and a full head of dark wavy hair, Richard reached over and shook Josie's hand. "Here," Richard said, handing each of the women a menu. "There's still time to order."

Chris and Josie sat down and studied their menus for a few minutes. "Uh," Josie put the menu down and stood up. "Actually, I need to use the restroom. If the waitress comes could you order me a burger, well-done, and a glass of the pinot?"

"I'll have the same." Chris stood up too. "By the way, we're Josie and Chris, roommates from San Francisco." Josie smiled at Richard and he smiled back.

Chris leaned over to Josie as they walked to the rest room. "One nice thing about this cycling stuff is that it's pretty easy to check out their equipment. Bike shorts don't leave much to the imagination you know." She elbowed Josie. "Check out that guy." The women giggled.

"Geeze Chris. You're incorrigible."

Josie was new to the city, and her roommate Chris suggested they do something to meet men. After several years of working on ships and living overseas, Josie had finally moved back to the states when her father had had a heart attack.

"I won't live forever you know," he told her from his hospital bed. "And you're no spring chicken."

"What are you trying to say, Dad?" She'd asked him, even though she knew what he was trying to say. She'd been hung up on her college boyfriend for years and had tried to keep up a futile long distance romance with him while he was busy dating other women on the side.

"What I'm trying to tell you Josephine, is that it's about time you started dating again. Meet a guy. Get married. Your mother was nineteen when she married me."

"Thanks, Dad. Let's just get straight to the point why don't we? Way to put pressure on me." Josie sighed but she knew he was right. She'd been out of college for several years, and at twenty-seven it was time to finally get over Ethan and find someone new.

The two roommates had just sat down and started eating their food when Josie noticed several of the other riders standing up, stretching and putting on their helmets. Richard and Bruce had finished eating and were talking about bikes.

"So what do you do?" Richard turned to Josie and smiled. "I'm an engineer. I work in the city. I lived overseas for a few years and worked on ships for a time. Then I decided to move to San Francisco."

"What about you?" Josie asked.

"I'm a native San Franciscan but I grew up on the Peninsula. I work in the south bay but I live in the city." Richard stood up and stretched. "Sorry to run. Nice meeting you ladies." He fished around in his wallet for something.

"Are you guys leaving already? We just got here." Chris asked between bites. Richard handed Josie his business card.

"Here's my number. Do you have a card?"

"Sorry, I left my purse in the car," Josie apologized.

"Are you listed in the club registry?" He asked.

"Yes, I think so. We're new though."

"I'll find you. We're both in the city - let's go out for a drink sometime," Richard suggested.

"I'd like that," Josie told him, smiling flirtatiously. The men walked away and got on their bikes. As they caught up with the pack and rode back down the driveway, Richard turned briefly and gave Josie a little wave before riding off. Josie watched as Richard's bright blue cycling shirt disappeared around the bend. She waved for the waitress, still gulping down her food. "Can we have our check? We need to get going," Josie said, suddenly in a hurry to catch up.

"All paid for ladies, those guys took care of it."

"Really – they paid for our lunch?" Chris and Josie looked at each other. "The guy in the blue shirt paid when I took the order." The waitress shrugged.

"That was nice," Chris said. "And the whole tight shorts thing is nice." She sipped her drink. "But other than that, this single cycling thing is a total bust," Chris concluded. The women watched as the few remaining riders got on their bikes and left.

"Oh, I don't know. All it takes is one. The right one. Anyway, I kind of like that guy, Richard," Josie mused out loud as she sipped her wine.

"Are you going to call him?" Chris asked.

"No, I don't think so. I'll wait, I have a feeling I'll hear from him though." Josie smiled.

⤳ 13 ⤶

A jowly, heavily made up woman in her late fifties sat behind a dark polished desk and silently tapped her pen on her leg as she waited impatiently for Josie to start talking. This was a free thirty minute consult, and Wendy Pepper was taking a loss on her valuable time. Still, these things often brought in new clients. It was the cost of doing business.

"I took out a restraining order against my husband." Josie began tentatively, looking for a reaction from the attorney. The attorney motioned for her to continue. "He abused our children. Especially our daughter," she continued. "We had a hearing last week and the judge said we need a custody evaluator. My husband has an attorney. I didn't even know if I wanted a divorce but I had to protect my kids. I was interviewed by a CPS investigator. She said I could lose my kids." Josie stopped and looked at the attorney.

"When you say abuse what do you mean? Did he make marks on them? Was there sexual abuse? Do you have any proof that he abused them? How old were the kids when this happened? Did you call CPS yourself or did someone turn you in?" Wendy leaned forward as she flipped open her notebook and started taking notes on a yellow pad.

"My daughter reported the abuse to her teacher. She's seven and my son is going on three. After she told her teacher, the whole thing basically snowballed. One day I was living my normal life, and the next I was being investigated by Child Protective Services.

My husband was always hitting them, shoving them and yelling at them. One time, my son's face was bruised when he shoved a door in his face. My husband said that was an accident though. He always says the same thing when I confronted him about it. He always said 'you can't prove it.' He never denies doing it – he just says I can't prove it. I'm not sure about any sexual stuff. Lately, he's been going into the bathroom when our daughter is taking a bath and urinating in front of her. I caught him doing that several times. Our house has four bathrooms and he could have just as easily used any of the others. I got really upset whenever I saw him do that." Josie stopped and watched as Wendy continued to write.

"What did your husband do when you confronted him about exposing himself? Did you tell CPS about that?" Wendy typed the name Bain into the court website and pulled up the docket. She saw that Richard Bain was represented by Adam Wiener.

"Whenever I confronted him about doing that he said nothing and just ran out of the room," Josie continued. "It happened several times. Once Phoebe told me 'Daddy touched my wee-wee' and I wrote that down in my log. I didn't confront him about it. I did put that in the restraining order, though. I didn't think to tell the CPS investigator because she never asked about anything sexual. I just answered her questions." Josie looked around at the spacious office with the thick carpets and modern art on the walls, as Wendy flipped through several pages of notes.

"Okay," Wendy continued. "What is your financial situation? Do you work? What does your husband do?" She glanced at the tall, slender, nicely dressed woman sitting nervously with her hand bag on her lap.

Wendy felt a tinge of contempt for Josie. She was probably a house-wife living in a million-dollar home in Loranda, who wanted out of a bad marriage. The child abuse may be real, but she wouldn't be able to prove it, so it would go nowhere in court. It wouldn't be the first time some housewife had come into her office alleging child abuse against her husband, when she really just wanted out of a bad marriage. Wendy looked over at the thirty-something woman with blond streaks in her hair. She was pretty good at predicting what a client was worth to her, and Josie looked to her like a twenty thousand dollar pay day, maybe more.

"I stopped working almost three years ago. I didn't plan to stop working though. I have an engineering degree and I used to make more money than my husband. I had complications during my last pregnancy, and somehow during the time I was off work my license expired. I found the renewal notice under a pile of stuff in my hus-band's office after it was already too late to renew my license. I know my husband sabotaged my career, but even though he did that he also seemed angry that I wasn't working and was staying home with our kids. It's like you can't please him. When I confronted him about hiding my license renewal he didn't deny that either. He never denies anything. He just said 'your license is your responsibility' and walked out of the room.

I tried to appeal, but the state board wouldn't renew it," Josie con-tinued. "So now I can't go back to work until I retake the license exam, and even then it will be hard to get a job. The exam is pretty grueling, and I don't think I'll be able to study for it again until my son is older. My husband doesn't help with the kids at all. He just makes things difficult for us. I have investments from before I was married, and I helped my husband get a better paying job around the same time that I left my job. He's in IT." Josie paused again.

"We have a house in Loranda that we bought together about nine years ago, and it has about a half-million dollars of equity in it now. I also maxed out my IRA every year while I was working. My husband has an IRA also. Last month my husband took all the money out of our checking account as soon as he moved out, and the only income I have is from my investments, and some money my mother is going to loan me. We were living mostly on my husband's income and now he's keeping all of it. He also has a lot of money available from his family – a lot more than I have from my family." Josie stopped talking as Wendy continued to write.

"All I want is to get my fair share of the house, and to take the kids to Montana. I don't care about child support or spousal support. If I get my half of the equity in the house, I'll be fine. I have pretty good income from my Montana investments. It's not enough to stay in the Bay Area, but it's enough to live up there for the time being. When my kids are a little older I plan to go to grad school and get going on a new career." Josie paused again. "So what are my chances of moving up there with the kids?"

Wendy put her pen down and looked at Josie. "What you're asking for is called a move-away, and I'll tell you flat out that they are frowned on by the courts. I've had clients ask, and I've never had one succeed. But, I'll put it in the motion. I strongly advise you not to give up child support. Assuming you get primary custody, there's nothing stopping your husband from filing for custody again in a few months, and if he got custody he'd get child support from you. Do you really believe he'd give up child support from you, if he was entitled to it? When it comes to custody and support, nothing is carved in stone. It can change at any time. Your kids are still young. Wait until they're teenagers, you'll need all the child support you can get. Summer camps, car insurance, clothing, it all adds up."

Wendy leaned forward in her chair and got down to business. "My rate is three hundred an hour and my paralegal bills at one-fifty an hour. I need a five thousand dollar retainer. I see your husband has retained Adam Weiner. I'd call Weiner a pit bull attorney, but I prefer not to insult an entire breed of dog." Wendy chuckled at her own joke.

"He'll contest the abuse claims since you can't prove anything, so it may work against you in court. I'm not saying I agree, I'm just telling you how it is. Good chance the judge will think you're another pampered housewife who made up false allegations of abuse in order to get the jump on custody. That's how these things work. Weiner will smear you in court with that. You said CPS is investigating – have they issued a report yet?" Wendy asked.

"No, I haven't heard about any report. This all happened before the holidays – a few weeks ago. Mr. Weiner has already smeared me in court, Ms. Pepper. He told the judge I was trying to perform a 'parent-ectomy' on my husband. I can't believe this could end up going against me in court – I mean everyone, from the CPS investigator, to Phoebe's teacher, to my therapist, said I had to get him to move out. He refused to move out, and he said if I moved back to Montana with the kids he'd have me arrested. I even warned him in advance that I'd get a restraining order. I don't know what else I was supposed to do." Josie was exasperated and distraught at the idea that she'd followed the advice of people in positions of authority, only to find out that it could all end up working against her.

"Do you think there's any chance we can settle this quickly? I really don't have a lot of money to spend on attorney fees. We don't even have a college fund for our kids," Josie asked, nervous about having to come up with so much money.

"Well, if I take the case I'll reach out to Weiner. I've worked with him before. It's possible they'll settle quickly, but it all depends on the client. Sometimes these guys are so angry that they'll spend hundreds of thousands of dollars and take it all the way to trial. It's hard to say."

Josie felt queasy. "Hundreds of thousands of dollars?" She stammered. Richard was always so cheap about everything they did as a family. On the rare occasion that they did go on vacation, it was usually to go backpacking or to the Bain family cabin. He seldom spent money on her or the kids. Their first Christmas together he hadn't even bothered to get Josie a gift, and she'd left him for two days because of it. She even thought of ending the marriage over it. Before she agreed to come back to him, she made him buy her a very expensive necklace. He'd made a good first impression on her years earlier during their brief courtship, but after they were married she realized he was actually cheap and stingy. Because he was so tight-fisted, Josie wanted to believe he'd never spend that much money on attorneys.

"Oh yeah," Wendy said. "I've had cases go well over two hundred thousand. Most of them settle before that. It just depends. I think the housing market has peaked. I'll add a motion to get the house on the market as soon as possible. Once the proceeds from the house are sitting in escrow we'll have a better chance of settling this." She jotted more notes.

"So, it looks like I'll be available to take the case." Wendy turned from her computer screen and slid a three-page contract across the desk for Josie to sign. "After your retainer check clears, I'll file the paperwork for a wage garnishment, so you have some money coming in. Then I'll write a letter to Weiner and put out some feelers about a quick settlement. Don't get your hopes up though. It looks like we'll also need to confer about a custody evaluator."

Wendy closed her notebook and walked Josie to the door of her office – precisely thirty minutes after the consultation had begun. "I look forward to representing you." Wendy shook Josie's hand as she held the door open for her to leave.

∽ 14 ∾

Josie walked barefoot on the soft earth, following the winding trail through a thick forest. Her long flowing hair framed her face and she wore a pale deerskin dress that fell to her knees. Her young son was on her back, with his arms around her neck and his head on her shoulder. He was bundled in a warm blanket that was tied snuggly to her body. She held a beautiful stick of smooth dark wood in one hand and Phoebe's small hand in the other. The night was clear and a full moon lit their way.

She came to a clearing and saw a fork in the trail. One branch led twisting and curving into the dense forest, while the other led out to an open landscape dotted with boulders and scattered trees. Josie turned around and saw a large grizzly bear towering over her. She remained calm and silent as he spoke.

"Go where the land is open and the ground is cool. Your husband will follow his own path. It is full of pain and torment. You will follow yours. Worry not."

The bear stepped back into the darkness, and Josie looked over at the twisted trail that lead deep into the forest. Richard stood on the forested trail, bent over at the waist and flailing his arms above his head, as if he was being attacked from above. He crept along his path, slowly and painfully, oblivious to Josie and the children.

Josie turned towards the open trail and held the polished stick in the air, high over her head. She watched as the end of the stick was suddenly struck by a bolt of lightning and she felt the electricity surge through her body. She saw the brief flicker of a halo silhouetting her and the children. Dropping the stick onto the soft earth she pulled Phoebe close and started down her path.

Curled up on her mother's sofa, Josie snored softly as Valerie and Austen entered the condo. She'd returned early from her meeting with the lawyer and had fallen into a deep sleep. Austen ran over to the couch, and climbed on his still-sleeping mother. Josie sat up. Her mouth was dry, her head was throbbing, and her hair was a mess. Austen climbed into her lap and hugged her. She kissed his head and closed her eyes.

"How did it go with the lawyer today, dear?" Valerie started putting away the groceries in her small kitchen.

"Wow, I'm exhausted. I haven't been sleeping well lately." Josie ran her fingers through her hair. "Oh yes, the attorney. I have a contract to sign. I need a five thousand dollar retainer. She'll start filing paper-work right away. She said she'd get his wages garnished for family support. She also said we need to get the house on the market as soon as possible," Josie said wearily.

"Where will you go if you sell the house?" Valerie asked, alarmed at the thought of her daughter moving away.

"I don't know right now. I just know that I can't afford to keep it. Even if I start studying for the engineering exam today, they only give it twice a year and it would be at least a year before I could conceivably be working again. The lawyer's right, the house has to be sold." Josie had mixed feelings about the house anyway. It was a beautiful house, and represented everything she'd worked so hard for, but it was also the place where there'd been so many tears and so much unhappiness for herself and the kids.

"Maybe we can move to Montana. I don't know. We can't very well squeeze in here with you. No matter where we go in the Bay Area, we'll be in worse schools, possibly much worse. I looked up the schools in our old Montana neighborhood and they're all top rated. We could do a lot worse – after all I got a good education growing up there. Going to Montana and taking over one of my apartments may be my best bet if the court allows it."

"Well, we can talk about it later Josie. There are a lot of options. I'll go to the bank this afternoon and take out money for your retainer. You'll need to open a new bank account right away. You also need to start putting your investment checks into a separate account. Do you want some lunch first?"

"Yes, I know mother. I've been meaning to do that to. I'll go now. I'm too upset to eat anything anyway." Josie grabbed her shoes and purse and left, with Austen trailing behind her.

$$\infty \ 15 \ \infty$$

Josie poured coffee for herself and her neighbor, Kate, before sitting down on the living room couch. Kate was perched on the edge of the hearth, and her three-year-old tow-headed son, Jasper, was building towers with Austen. Eight years younger than Josie, Kate had weathered her own recent divorce with the help of her wealthy parents.

"How am I supposed to know if this lawyer is any good before I hand over the money?" Josie asked. Kate had a law degree but had never used it.

"Did you get a referral?" Kate asked.

"Yes, I got a referral from the local bar association," Josie said, taking a sip of coffee. "She seems tough, and she knows Richard's attorney, so I guess that's good. But she also told me that the fact that CPS is investigating could end up being a disadvantage for me. She said the judge might actually think I fabricated the whole thing," Josie said, exasperated.

"I saw Richard yell at Phoebe and make her cry, but I never saw him hit her," Kate said. "Phoebe said things to me about her dad hurting her, and I know you told me that he did stuff when you weren't there. But basically, it's his word against Phoebe's word. I can give you a statement about what I know – if that helps. The attorney may be right though – it becomes a 'he said she said.' Did she say anything about a custody evaluation?" Kate swept a strand of long blond hair away from her face.

"The lawyer didn't say much, but the judge said I'd need to come up with ten thousand dollars to hire an evaluator. Not sure how I'm supposed to make that happen." Josie stared at the two boys playing on the floor.

"So the judge isn't going to wait for the CPS report. He just ordered you guys to hire an evaluator?" Kate stood up and walked over to the couch.

"I hate to be the one to tell you this, Josie, but you're being fed into the ravenous jaws of the divorce industry. This is just the beginning. Chances are, you will deal with accountants and therapists and maybe even minor's counsel – all ordered by the judge and paid for by you and Richard. I was able to avoid that because Charles knew my family could out-spend him a thousand times over, and because I have a law degree. He pretty much just took what my dad offered him and went away. My dad was pretty generous though. What it really comes down to is that the person with the most money wins. Welcome to the justice system."

Kate sat down and looked Josie in the eye. Josie knew Kate had decided never to practice law, but this was the first time she'd really told Josie what she thought of the legal system. "Wow, Kate. How are ordinary people supposed to deal with this?"

"I don't know." Kate shrugged. "You're in the same position my ex was in, as far as your in-laws. Maybe Richard will make you a reasonable offer and you can start over somewhere else. I'm really sorry." Kate shook her head.

Josie stood up, agitated. "I don't know, Kate. I'm an engineer. I've never set foot in a law school in my life. But somehow I can't believe it's really all that bad. I did exactly what I was told to do, by someone with the authority to take my kids away. I had no choice. I had to protect them. It's like you're saying that no good deed goes unpunished. I really don't believe that. I don't believe the CPS investigator, and the teacher, and the therapist would all tell me I have to make Richard move out or risk losing my kids, only to have my efforts to protect the kids used against me. I mean it's positively evil," Josie said angrily.

"Maybe you're right, Josie." Kate stood up and took her son's hand. "I hope you're right. I think you did the right thing, for what it's worth. If Phoebe had to live with that abuse throughout her childhood, she'd a mess by the time she got to high school. And Austen would suffer too. So, no question you did the right thing. I'm willing to write a statement about what Phoebe said to me. But the fact remains, unless the kid ends up in the hospital with broken bones or third degree burns, the judge will disregard abuse allegations at best, and will actually think you fabricated them at worst. I would hire the attorney you talked to. It sounds like she knows how the system works, and that's what you need right now. Richard also knows how the system works. He knew he could abuse Phoebe, and as long as he pulled his punches and she didn't end up with any noticeable marks or injuries, he'd get away with it. Most likely he also knew that if you ever reported it, he could turn around and use it to make you look bad. You're right, it's evil." Kate knelt down to tie Jasper's shoe.

"And even if Phoebe had some marks on her, you'd have to have taken her to the doctor, and taken photos, and logged all the details – and even then he could just say it was an accident. Kids get hurt all the time," Kate continued. "My kids always have little bruises and scrapes. It proves nothing. And don't be surprised when he goes for full custody." Kate scooped up Jasper and opened the front door to leave. "One last thing, Josie, please don't blame the messenger. I'm your friend, I'm on your side, and I'm just trying to help."

Josie sat down at the kitchen table and stared at the wall. *Engineers fix things. They solve problems. They find solutions. I've always been able to solve problems – that's what I do,* Josie thought to herself. There may have been a better solution to the problem of Richard abusing the kids but she didn't know what it was. In any case, she was now on to a new problem. She had to find the money to fight Richard and his family. She had to find money for the custody evaluator. Richard's lawyer had already told the judge that Richard was a loving father, and that she'd made the whole thing up. The misinformation campaign had already begun. There were no computer programs to help her with this problem. There was no supply catalog where she could find the right component to fix this. There was no blue print to go by.

Josie went into the office and sifted through several days of unopened mail. She set aside the credit card offers that arrived daily, and opened the statement from her property management company in Montana. She picked up the phone and called her property manager.

"Hi, it's Josephine Bain." Josie looked in the desk drawer and found a pen and note pad. "I just wanted to let you know that Richard and I are separated and I'll be handling all the decisions about the properties from now on. I know he's been dealing with it lately, but the properties are actually mine and I don't want him involved with them anymore. My computer is down right now but when I get it back up I'll follow up with an email. Thanks." Josie left a message and hung up the phone.

She found the monthly check from the property management and put it in her purse. Then she opened up the credit card offers one by one and looked them over carefully. She'd always been sparing in her use of credit cards. She and Richard had two cards between them and paid them off every month. Josie took the cards out of her wallet and called the toll free numbers. Richard had already charged new furniture to one of the cards. Josie asked both companies to remove her name from the accounts.

She laid out all the credit card offers on the kitchen table and went through them one by one, looking for the best deals. She filled out the best two offers and put them in the envelopes. She stuffed the envelopes into her purse and picked up Austen.

"Come on, sweetie. Mommy has to go to the bank now." Austen squirmed and fussed. "I know you're tired of having to run around with Mommy so much, but after we get done at the bank we'll go to the library and pick out some new books."

Josie endorsed the check from the property management company along with the check her mother had given her, and passed them to the banker. "I need to open a new account and I'd also like to open a line of credit," she told the earnest young man. "No problem, Mrs. Bain, you have excellent credit," he said as he worked at his computer. "If you're married your husband will also need to sign. How much would you like?"

"Oh, well in that case, never mind. We're getting divorced. It's just that I have all these expenses right now. How about getting the house refinanced? We have a fifteen-year loan and everything would be easier if it was a thirty year." Josie paused.

"I'm sorry, Mrs. Bain. Without your husband's signature you won't be able to refinance through us." The banker shook his head apologetically as he finished setting up her new account. She thanked him and left.

"I took my name off the joint credit cards and opened a new bank account." Josie leaned against the counter in her mother's small kitchen while Valerie prepared dinner. Phoebe sat at the kitchen table doing her second grade homework, while Austen stared at the TV in the living room.

"Did you deposit the check I gave you? My broker told me I have to start taking money out of my IRA every year. I was going to give some of it to you anyway so you could start a college fund for the kids. Now it will have to go to the attorney." Valerie took a tray of warm rolls out of the oven.

"Yes, I put it in the bank today. I really appreciate you helping me, Mom. I still can't believe this is happening." Josie grabbed some plates to set the table. "I'll mail the check and the contract to the attorney tomorrow. I also filled out new credit card applications. Everyone keeps telling me how much this is all going to cost and I have to be ready."

After dinner, Josie and Valerie sat on the back deck and talked quietly. The kids were inside watching TV.

"Kate came over today. She basically said I was toast - in so many words. I guess she was trying to help, but she made it seem like I just need to give up or something. She basically said the same thing the attorney told me: there's a good chance the judge would think I made the whole thing up and hold it against me, blah, blah, blah. I guess it all comes down to the custody evaluation. I don't even know what I could have done differently. Phoebe said what she said, and the teacher and principle did what they did, and the social worker did what she did, and all of it happened without me even being involved. I feel like the whole thing was beyond my control."

"I keep going over it in my head, and I wonder if there was something I did wrong – some way I could have handled this whole thing better. But apparently Richard was a step ahead of me the whole time. I feel like there should be a better solution to the problem, besides having to borrow a ton of money and waste it all on attorneys and evaluators and the rest." Josie stared into the blackness of the canyon just beyond her mother's deck.

"There is nothing you could have done differently," Valerie said. "Richard is basically a criminal. He has a criminal mentality. He always told you that you couldn't prove anything. What that really means is that in his mind it didn't matter what he did, it only mattered whether somebody else could prove it. Criminals get away with committing crimes against unsuspecting people because we don't think like them. We don't see it coming because it never occurs to us that someone would do that. I've always wondered what you saw in him."

Josie gave her mother an exasperated look. "I'm sorry, Josie. We've been through that dozens of times. You always make a joke out of it and say 'it seemed like a good idea at the time,' and I guess it doesn't really matter, because if you hadn't married him I wouldn't have my beautiful grandchildren, so let's not even go there," Valerie rambled. "It's just that he's so different from Ethan. Your father and I really liked him," she added gratuitously.

"Do you remember when I came back from New Zealand after Dad had his first heart attack?" Josie turned to her mother. "Well, he sat right there in his hospital bed and basically pressured me to hurry up and find a guy. I remember exactly what he said – he said, and I quote: 'Josephine, you are no spring chicken.' I mean, back then I actually was a spring chicken. I guess he wanted grandchildren and he knew my brothers were in no big hurry to get married."

"Sweetheart, your father wasn't the same after his heart attack. It really pulled the rug right out from under him. Anyway, let's not talk about this anymore. I'm sorry your father pressured you…"

"That's okay, Mom. It doesn't matter anyway, you can't change the past."

Josie stood abruptly, walked into the living room and turned off the TV. "It's time to go kids. Phoebe has school tomorrow." She picked up Austen, who was starting to fall asleep and grabbed the diaper bag, while Phoebe put her things into her backpack.

"Bye-bye Grandma," Phoebe said, giving Valerie a hug.

"I'll call in the morning, Mom. Things always feel worse in the evening." Josie walked out the door with the kids.

16

Josie sat on the bench next to the laurel tree in her garden. It was the middle of winter, and the walkway was covered with piles of soggy leaves. The laurel was the only part of the original landscaping left and was by far the biggest tree in the yard. She and Richard had torn out the original landscaping, which had consisted mostly of overgrown cypress trees full of rodent nests surrounded by weeds and spindly rose bushes.

They'd put in a variety of fruit trees, berry bushes and raised beds full of potatoes and asparagus plants. Working in the garden was one of the things they had in common during the first years of their marriage. They worked without a plan, just putting in whatever they felt like. Richard liked grapes so he'd built a grape arbor. The tiny blueberry bushes she'd planted were over five feet tall now. And the fig tree she'd insisted on planting was now a thing of beauty.

It was on a mid-December evening the year before last that Josie had come home from her father's hospital bedside, distraught and speechless. She knew he was dying but she was unable to process it.

She'd brushed past Richard as he held their crying toddler, hurried into the master bedroom and closed the door behind her. Without bothering to get undressed she curled up in bed and cried herself into a deep and restless sleep.

The dream she had that night was unlike any she'd ever had, before or since. The rheostat of her unconscious mind had been turned up high, and the vividness of the dream seared itself into her mind's eye. The image itself was very simple: She was in her bedroom looking out of an imaginary window at the twenty-foot-tall laurel tree. She watched calmly as the tree was suddenly and violently split in half. That was all she remembered of the dream.

The following morning Richard woke her early and told her two things: Her mother had phoned at midnight to tell her that her father had died, and the laurel tree in the yard was split down the middle.

"Oh no," Josie said, sitting up in bed. "He was in a coma last night. I stayed with him for hours. They had him on a breathing machine and my mom thought he was probably already gone and that the machine was breathing for him. I felt his hand one last time and it was cold. That's when I left." A shiver went down her spine. "Please take care of the kids today, Richard. I just want to be alone." Her voice was sad and her face was wet with tears. Richard stood up to leave.

"Oh, wait." Josie stopped him. "What did you say about the tree? That it split in half or something? What happened to it? Was it windy last night? How did it just split in half?" Josie dabbed at her eyes and face with a tissue.

"I don't know," Richard said matter-of-factly. "It was strange. There was no wind last night, just a little rain. Nothing that would knock down a tree like that. I heard something and went out to look. The tree was split and part of it was lying on the roof of the shed." Richard shook his head and shrugged. "I'll take the chain saw out there later and cut it down." He started to leave.

"Richard, my father died last night. Aren't you going to say anything? Tell me something like you're sorry or something?" Josie sat on the side of the bed looking at him. "Your dad never liked me, Josie." He shrugged. "But I'll watch the kids today if you want." He left the room.

Josie went to the French doors and looked into the garden at the split tree. It had been the only tree in the yard that provided shade during the blazing hot summers. The lower trunk was intact, but about half of the canopy had split off where the two main branches rose from the trunk. .

"Richard, could you please come back here for a minute?" Josie called down the hall. Richard came back into the room, scowling. "Can you at least try to be nice, Richard, my dad died last night. Can't you at least have a little sympathy?" She said, anger rising in her throat. "Is that why you called me back here?" Richard asked.

"No. I want to talk about the tree. I don't want you to cut it down. My father died last night and now you are going to cut down my favorite tree. It's the only tree that gives any shade when this town turns into a blast furnace every summer. Please don't cut it down. It will live. Just remove the part that split off and leave the rest. The part that's still there is the part that shades our corner of the house anyway." Josie's eyes were red and swollen with grief.

"Okay," Richard said. "Fine by me. Less work. I'll just cut up the dead branch and stuff it into the green can. I doubt it will live though. Any more requests, Josie?" He added, mockingly.

"Wow, Richard. How would you like it if someone in your family died and I was snarky to you? Anyway, please just leave me alone."

The last time she saw her father, her mother and one of her brothers were already at the hospital. They all agreed to give each other a few moments alone with him to say goodbye. When her turn came she sat with him quietly for a few minutes before beginning to speak softly, her voice breaking.

She told him about her life with Richard. It was a deathbed confession in reverse. Her father lay in a coma, silent except for the sound of the ventilator, while she sobbed and blurted out things about her marriage that she'd never shared with him before he became ill – when he might have been able to help her. She told him that Richard was a bad man, and an abusive father to her children – her own father's only and much beloved grandchildren. She said she wished he was healthy and strong again, and could somehow help her. She stared out the rain-streaked window at a blinking blue neon sign that said "Serendipity." She looked at his unlined face, still handsome and composed even on his deathbed.

"You didn't raise us with any religion Dad, but I want to believe you will be somewhere in the universe. I want you to know that you will always live in my thoughts and in my memories, and I will tell my children about you." She went into the hallway and hugged her mother before going home.

Josie sat on the stone bench opposite the laurel tree in her back yard, thinking back to the night her father died. A faint breeze rustled the leaves and a dog barked in the distance. She felt her father's presence whenever she sat there. Closing her eyes, she began to speak softly.

"I know you're still here Dad. It was you who split this tree, wasn't it?" With her eyes still closed she envisioned her father sitting down beside her. "Things really fell apart after you died. Richard moved a couple months ago. Well, actually I forced him to move out," Josie explained calmly.

"I knew something strange happened the night you died, Dad. I had a very strange dream and I'll never forget it. The next morning, Richard told me that this tree had split in half. He wanted to cut it down, but I stopped him. He couldn't figure out what had happened. There wasn't any wind at all that night. But somehow, I knew. I knew it was you. Somehow, I knew it was a message from you." Josie saw the image of her father as he smiled and nodded.

"A few months after you died, I found a book on dream interpretation. I looked up what it meant to dream that a tree had been split in half. It means that a family is going to break up." She opened her eyes and gazed at the tree, tall and healthy, with new shoots growing out of the split trunk.

"When I was little you told me a story I will never forget. It was about a man who could make something out of nothing. He started with a beautiful suit, and little by little things kept happening to him and he lost parts of his prized possession until all he had left was one button. But he never gave up and somehow he made the whole suit again from that one little button. The moral of the story was that you can always make something out of nothing."

Josie continued speaking in a soft voice. "I always wanted to be the kind of person who could make something out of nothing. Well now I have to. I'm losing what I have and I have to make it all back but I don't have my job or my license. I am going to have to make something out of nothing." She paused and blinked back a tear.

"The only time I mentioned Richard's meanness to you, you told that I couldn't make a silk purse from a sow's ear, and you were right. You were always right about Richard. You were right not to like him, Dad," Josie said, as tears filled her eyes.

"I just came out here today to tell you and to tell myself that I'm going to be okay. I made something of my life before I met Richard, and I'll do it again. Even if I lose everything I've worked for, even if I get down to that one last button, I will find a way to build something beautiful with it. Richard and his family can take everything away but I know I can make something out of nothing because you taught me that I could." Josie wiped a tear from her eye and glanced over at the empty bench beside her.

⤲ 17 ⤳

"This is war Josie, and we're going to have to man the battle stations. Remember – never talk to Richard or his family again. It's a basic rule of warfare: don't drop ammunition behind enemy lines." Alice paced in front of the picture windows looking out into the garden of her Montana house. She'd been calling Josie daily to give her moral support. They were friends from college and had stayed close. Alice had grown up in a beautiful Southern California beach town, the daughter of an admiral. As soon as college ended, she'd headed for the Rocky Mountains and never looked back. She was happy in her laid-back mountain town, with her boyfriend, her bungalow and her dogs.

"Everyone said I should have gone to law school, but except for Tim, I basically hate all lawyers. And divorce lawyers are the worst of all," Alice said with disdain. Josie held the phone in the crook of her neck while she scrambled eggs and buttered toast in her Bay Area kitchen a thousand miles away.

"I really appreciate all your support, Alice. It means a lot to me. The attorneys agreed on an evaluator. We each have to pay seventy-five hundred dollars, but he accepts credit cards – isn't that nice of him?" Josie set two plates on the table, and poured coffee for herself. "The bank turned me down for a line of credit, saying I need Richard's signature. But lucky me I have a couple new credit cards. Forgive me, Alice, I'm in a crummy mood." She pushed Austen's chair in, and sat down to eat, still holding the phone in one hand.

"It's an industry, Josie. It's a corrupt, money-driven industry. And unless you've been through it, you have no idea how it works," Alice said bitterly.

"I'm finally getting clued in about this stuff," Josie said. "I can't believe how naïve I was. I thought the judge would just make a decision about custody, but no. They just tell you to empty out your bank account and hire an evaluator. Of course Richard beat me to the bank account."

Josie stared at the bills and legal papers spread out across her kitchen table. "The good news is my attorney said the wage garnishment should start soon. The bad news is that the amount he is supposed to give us isn't even enough to pay the mortgage."

"So much for the college fund. Phoebe and Austen better get scholarships." Josie leaned across the table to gently stop Austen from folding one of the legal documents into a paper airplane.

"You'll recover, Josie. You know how to make something of yourself. You'll be fine. The only thing Richard knows how to do is spend his mother's money and take advantage of other people." Alice looked out the window at the steadily falling snow and the gray Montana sky.

"I don't know. I'm pushing forty, I have two young kids and no job," Josie sighed. "My cousin is a stock broker in Los Angeles. She says she's seen a lot of women go from living in mansions, to living in two bedroom apartments after a divorce." Josie shook her head.

"Anyway, I have to go. I have an appointment with the attorney in an hour. I'll call you later."

"I called you here to go over a few things for the custody eval and the settlement proposal." Wendy greeted Josie at the door of her office and briskly sat down at her desk as her client took a seat opposite her. She slid a legal document across to Josie. "The evaluator is Dr. Stokes. He does a lot of these. He tends to favor the dad, but the other two options were even worse." Wendy looked over her glasses at Josie.

"Do you have some makeup and a nice casual dress to wear, Mrs. Bain?" Wendy inquired.

"I have makeup, but I never have time to put it on anymore," Josie shrugged.

"Well, use it. And do something about your hair – your gray is starting to show. And make sure the house is clean, but leave a few toys around. You need to make a good appearance. This evaluation stuff is a lot of hooey. But Stokes is a guy, so get rid of the gray and put on some lipstick. And wear a skirt." Wendy paused. "You need to be the wholesome movie mom"

"He'll do a full psych evaluation, too. Don't worry about that. Just answer the questions honestly. He's mainly trying to see if either of you is a total nut ball." Wendy shuffled some of her papers.

"We finally got the CPS report. There were no details – it just said the abuse allegations were unfounded." Wendy looked at Josie and shrugged.

"I'm not surprised. This is usually what happens in these cases. No broken bones. No hospital reports. No police reports. That's how it works."

"Wow. I'm in shock," Josie stammered and leaned back in her chair. "You mean the social worker told me I could lose my kids if I continued to live with Richard, and basically broke up my marriage, and now she's saying, 'Oh never mind?'" Josie was incredulous. "Oh my God. Can they do that? Can they break up someone's marriage, and then just throw them under the bus when the thing ends up in court?" Josie's heart was racing.

"Let's be honest, Mrs. Bain. If what you say is true the marriage was over. Your kids were being hurt – regardless of what the CPS report says." Wendy tried to console her client.

"I can file some paperwork and try to get a copy of the actual interview she conducted with your daughter. Dr. Stokes is familiar with how CPS works. If your daughter said something damaging about her dad to the social worker, we can give a copy of the report to Stokes. It might help your custody case. Also, we filed for joint custody, but your husband filed for sole custody. It always looks better to the evaluator when a party files for joint custody rather than sole custody. Unfortunately, though, the fact that you're asking to take the kids out of state doesn't look so good. Most evaluators take a dim view of that." Wendy paused to let Josie respond.

"It's not like I have much choice, Ms. Pepper. I have no job. I have no license to get a job. I can't afford to stay in the Bay Area, and I have a nice place to stay in Montana with excellent schools for the kids. What can I do to convince Dr. Stokes? Besides dying my hair and wearing a dress and trying not to look like a nut job, that is?"

"You can start writing, Mrs. Bain. But remember, the other party gets a copy of everything. My advice is to stay positive. Write about what a wonderful place Montana is, and how great it is for children. Paint a picture of the house, the neighborhood, the school, the whole environment. You can put stuff in there about Richard, but if it's really negative it might actually hurt you. One of the criteria they use is that they want the parent who is more likely to share the kids to get primary custody. That's why is looks bad for Richard to ask for sole custody. Frankly I'm surprised Weiner didn't talk him out of it."

"He probably tried, but you can't tell Richard anything. Probably even his lawyer can't tell him anything." Josie paused. "Is there anything else I can do to help my case?"

"Ask your friends, co-workers, family and neighbors to start writing. They can send everything to me, and I'll look it over before I send a copy to Stokes and Weiner. Each side has to share what they have with the other side. It looks better to have other people talk about the abuse. If anyone you know actually witnessed abuse, or if your kids reported it to anyone else, have that person write about it. Good chance Stokes will still ignore it, but it's worth a try. Meanwhile, I'll see if I can get a copy of the CPS interview." Wendy took out her legal pad and started to write.

"I need to go over the financials with you again, Mrs. Bain." Josie nodded. "When did you purchase the rental properties and what is the net monthly income? Have you had the properties appraised recently? If not, do you know the approximate values?"

"I bought them when I was in my early twenties, a few years before I married Richard. After I graduated from college I got a job working overseas. I was making good money and most of my living expenses were covered. My dad convinced me to buy rental properties in my hometown. Unfortunately, everyone in my family has left the state since then, but I still have a couple of friends there. It was a lot more affordable than trying to buy apartment buildings in the Bay Area." Josie paused as her attorney continued to write.

"The rental income fluctuates, but for the last couple years it was about one-third of our total monthly income. The property management company pays all the expenses and sends us a check every month. The properties are all in my name, but they used to send the check in both of our names. I called the management company and told them to make the checks out to me from now on. I also opened a new bank account and I no longer use our joint account," Josie said.

"So, before you separated you had the management company put the checks in both your names and you deposited the money in your joint account? Okay, so what about the value of the rental properties? Also, tell me about the Loranda house."

"We bought the Loranda house together about six months after we married. It's been going up every year since we bought it. We always said if it gets to a million we'll sell. Well, houses just like it are selling for over a million dollars now. I'm worried, because I think the market is going to pop. It's just gone so high so fast. I really want to sell it. We have several hundred thousand dollars in equity in it and half of it is mine."

"As for the rentals, I don't really keep track of the market up there. I know it's gone up a lot but not as much as here. All my rental properties together are probably worth about what the house in Loranda is worth." Josie leaned back in her chair.

"Okay. I've filed a motion to get the house sold. I agree with you about the market, by the way. I think it's peaked and at best will level off. At worst it could fall quite a bit. As far as the rental properties," Wendy continued. "Even though you bought them before your marriage, you had the checks made out to you and to Richard and you deposited them in your joint account. This gives Richard a claim on them, I'm afraid." Wendy looked at Josie.

"How is that possible? I bought them before I even knew him! I only had the checks made out to both of us because I thought that's what married couples do! My parents never had separate money! I'm quite sure Richard's parents never had separate money! What does it mean as far as the divorce?" Josie said, her face starting to flush.

"It means that Weiner will ask the court to award some of the rental property to Richard. Good chance Richard doesn't really want the rental property, since it's in another state, but he can use it as leverage," Wendy told Josie.

"Leverage? Leverage for what?" Josie shook her head.

"Leverage for the Loranda house, Mrs. Bain. Instead of agreeing to sell the Loranda house and split the proceeds, he can offer to buy you out."

"He can't afford to buy me out, Ms. Pepper. I know his mother will give him money for the attorney but I doubt she'll hand him a few hundred thousand to buy my half of the house."

"That's where the rental properties come in, Mrs. Bain. He could ask the court to award him half of the amount that the rental properties increased in value during the marriage and then turn around and trade his share of those properties for your share of the Loranda house. That's if you're lucky. If you're not, then he'll ask for your share of the Loranda house plus one or more of your other properties."

Wendy watched as her client absorbed this news. "I know you acted in good faith by putting the money in your joint account and I'll definitely put that in the filing if this goes before the judge. But this is how these things work. You should have kept everything separate."

"So basically what you're saying is that if the rental properties doubled in value during our ten-year marriage, then he owns half of the increased value?" Josie punched some numbers into the calculator on her cell phone.

"Yes. That's right." Wendy answered.

"So that pretty much wipes out my share of the Loranda house. I can't believe this is how the law works. I found that house. I negotiated for that house. I paid for that house. I made more money than he did during most of our marriage. And now you're telling me I won't get anything from the house?"

"We can take it to court Mrs. Bain. But the judge will set the whole thing for trial and you'll have to pay a forensic accountant to look at all the numbers. You may be better off trying to settle," Wendy told her.

"So Richard hurts our children and CPS tells me to make him move out. Then the judge sees a restraining order and thinks I'm just making the whole thing up. And now I have to pay for a custody evaluation and grovel for the right to protect my children from an abuser. And I have to give him my half of the house or else he gets to have half of the property I owned years before I ever met him? This is unbelievable!"

"Mrs. Bain." Wendy put her pen down. "You married a rat bastard. Someday I'm going to write a field guide so that women like you can spot these guys. You see, it's a game for Richard. He gamed your marriage. I have to believe he had legal advice along the way. He probably consulted an attorney before and during the marriage. He knew the rules and used them against you. And we haven't even talked about the retirement funds yet."

"The retirement funds? What about the retirement funds?" Josie raised her voice.

"Please try to calm down, Mrs. Bain. I know this is hard, but in order to proceed with a settlement proposal I need to know about the pensions." Wendy flipped the page on her yellow pad.

"We both have IRA and 401K accounts." Josie began. "I put the maximum amount in mine until I left my job three years ago. I don't know about Richard. I know he has them, too." Josie kept punching numbers into her calculator as she talked.

"If you're lucky he kept funding his retirement accounts during the marriage," Wendy said. "I'm only saying that because I've seen this stuff before. A lot of times when guys like him get married later in life, they stop funding their IRA after the wedding. The wife, being younger, keeps socking money away in her accounts, though. Then, if there's a divorce, he gets half of her retirement funds and she gets nothing from his. Like I said, I've seen it before. It's straight from the rat bastard playbook. Anyway, I won't know the situation until I see his financials."

Josie wanted to run screaming from the room. Richard always did the taxes and kept the files for all the financial stuff. Josie realized that she had no idea if he had been putting money in his IRA and 401K during the marriage or not. She'd never thought to ask him. During one of their last fights, Richard told her that he'd get half of her property and half of her retirement accounts, but she hadn't believed him.

❧ 18 ❧

Josie set up two folding chairs next to the baseball diamond in one of Loranda's tree-lined parks. She handed Austen a box of raisins, and watched as Phoebe ran into the outfield before turning around to wave.

"The forecast said rain, but it looks like we'll get lucky," said Nancy, the mother of Phoebe's best friend as she set up her chair next to Josie. "Is Richard going to be here today?" She asked.

"He better not be. We have a restraining order in effect remember?" Josie pulled a sweater out of her bag and put it on. "I see his cousin, Janelle, is here though. That's her over there." Josie nodded in the direction of a tall dark-haired woman in her twenties walking over from the parking lot.

"Not sure why she's here. She lives in the city and we usually only see her during holidays at my mother-in-law's house. Richard's whole family has closed ranks against me. Janelle's brother came over to the house to rip me off right before Christmas. I let him in because he said he came to get some of Richard's things and then he went into the office when I wasn't looking and took all the files about the investments and IRAs. I'm pretty sure he did something to the computer, but by the time I figured it out there was nothing to do. He also brought Christmas presents, but when I handed them out on Christmas morning, it turned out that all the presents were for Austen. Not one of the presents from Richard or his family was for Phoebe."

"Wow, you never told me that, Josie. What a jerk. Poor Phoebe." Nancy watched as her daughter, Drew, ran onto the field with her team.

"We made it up to Phoebe. My mom came through and got her a new doll with all the accessories." Josie shrugged.

Richard's parents had put Janelle and her brother Andrew through college after their own father had disappeared when they were children. Janelle owed a debt of gratitude to Richard's family, and was happy to drive out from the city and give Austen a gift from his father. Along with the rest of Richard's family, she was outraged when she heard that Josie had filed a restraining order against her cousin. She knew he had a temper but she didn't believe he'd ever hurt the kids. She assumed that Josie had made the whole thing up. Spotting Josie and Austen, Janelle waved as she walked over with her chair slung over her shoulder.

"Hi, Austen!" Janelle squealed, completely ignoring Josie. "Wow, you're getting so big! Hey kiddo, it's me, your cousin Janny. I have something for you. Something from your Daddy. Your Daddy misses you a lot!" Janelle continued talking to the little boy in an awkward, high-pitched voice while she fumbled in her back pack. Austen squeezed closer to his mother and growled at Janelle as she pulled a small plastic bag from her pack and crouched down in the grass to get closer to him.

"Sweetie, do you remember Daddy's cousin, Janelle? Andrew's big sister? We see Janelle every year at Thanksgiving and Christmas. She won't hurt you sweetheart." Josie coaxed Austen as he made a low rumbling growl.

"What's wrong? Why's he growling?" Janelle asked, squinting at Josie. She reached her hand out to touch her cousin's young son then abruptly pulled it back. "Yow – Austen – what'd you do that for?" She shrieked, clasping the side of her hand. "He bit me, Josie. Your son bit me!" Janelle dropped the plastic bag on the ground and Austen grabbed it.

"Sorry Janelle." Josie pulled Austen onto her lap. "He does that sometimes. It's normal. I'll talk to him about it." Josie turned Austen around to face her and scolded him gently. "You must never do that, Austen. You hurt Janelle. You are not allowed to bite people. Do you understand?" Austen nodded somberly.

Janelle set up her chair a few feet from Josie's group. "That's too much! First he growls at me. Then he bites me - great parenting, Josie!" Janelle shook her head.

"You've never had kids Janelle so what do you know about parenting? It's normal behavior for a boy his age. It has nothing to do with parenting."

Josie turned back to her friend Nancy. "We call him dog boy." Josie said, laughing. "He growls, he bites, and one time I caught him with a few pieces of dog food in his mouth." Josie joked about it as Janelle set up her chair nearby. "Anyway, I told the therapist about it and she said some boys do it when they're scared." Josie gave Austen a squeeze.

As the inning ended Phoebe ran to the dugout with her team and put on a batter's helmet. "Look, Austen – Phoebe's up at bat!" Josie said, abruptly changing the subject. She pointed to Phoebe standing at home plate poised to hit the ball.

Phoebe's teammates clung to the dugout fence, and began chanting in unison: "EXTRA EXTRA READ ALL ABOUT IT, PHOEBE'S GONNA HIT THE BALL NO DOUBT ABOUT IT!"

The coach, a tall amiable man in his forties, stood halfway between the pitcher's mound and home plate and gently threw the softball in an underhand motion. Phoebe swung hard and connected with the slow-moving ball. Her coach barely managed to duck in time as Phoebe slammed a line drive right at his head. She dropped the bat and jogged towards first base. Phoebe was the team's best hitter but hated running the bases. In fact, she hated running period. It was her big downfall as an athlete.

Josie put Austen down and jumped to her feet. "Go, Phoebe! Run! Faster, Phoebe! You can do it! Keep running!" She yelled at her seven-year-old, as three girls on the other team chased and fumbled the ball around the outfield. Phoebe looked around and ran slowly to second, and then to third. "Good job, Phoebe!" Josie yelled again as Phoebe's teammates whooped and yelled for her to run home. Sitting back down, Josie pulled Austen onto her lap. "Booyah Mommy." Austen said, smiling at Josie. She gave him a fist bump and laughed. "That's right, Austen! Booyah!"

"Phoebe's pretty good," Janelle said, trying to join the group.

"I'm surprised you're here, Janelle." Josie turned to look at her. "You drove out from San Francisco just to watch a kid's softball game?" Josie unexpectedly felt a surge of anger towards Janelle.

"No offense Janelle, but we're on opposite teams now. And by the way, I know your brother Andrew ripped me off. He came over before Christmas and did something to crash the computer. There are a bunch of paper files missing too. And not bothering to bring Christmas presents for Phoebe? Leave a little kid off the Christmas list, just because she said something to her teacher? That says a lot about the Bain family, Janelle." Josie pointedly shifted her chair to talk to her friend Nancy, completely turning her back on the interloper.

"Really, Josie?" Nancy said nervously, suddenly finding herself in the middle of a family feud. "Girls let's just watch the game shall we?" Nancy suggested.

"You're right, Nance. I'm on edge, forgive me." Josie apologized. Phoebe and Drew came running over to the women.

"Did you see me, Austen? Did you see big sister hit the ball?" Phoebe gave her baby brother a fist bump and whooped "Booyah, Austen! That was fun!"

"We're thirsty did you bring water, Mom?" Both girls blurted out at the same time.

"Hey Phoebe, aren't you going to say hi to your favorite cousin?" Janelle put a hand on Phoebe's shoulder. Phoebe glanced at Janelle and shrugged, before grabbing a water bottle and running back to the dugout.

"Well, I'm out of here," Janelle announced as she stood and packed up her chair. "Thanks for the hospitality, Josie." She called over her shoulder as she left. She walked back to the parking lot, talking on her cell phone.

"What was that about?" Nancy asked.

"I don't know," Josie said. "All I want to do is enjoy being at my kid's game and Richard sends his minions out here to spy on me." Josie shrugged. "It turns out the whole thing really is just a game." She mused out loud. "Richard has been three steps ahead of me the whole time. The trouble is I didn't realize it was a game. If I had, then I would have done pretty well. I mean I've got game too. My bad, I thought this was a marriage. I never realized the whole thing was one big game," Josie said ruefully.

"You're starting to sound bitter, Josie." Nancy took a sip of water. "You're not even forty yet, you're still young. You can start over. I'm sorry about Richard. Live and learn. That's what we all do," Nancy consoled her friend.

"Okay, you're right. I don't want to be bitter. Anyway, as far as I'm concerned it's game on. He probably thinks its game over, but I'll show him." Josie forced a smile and took a sip of water.

"Just remember," Nancy told her friend "revenge is a dish best served cold."

❧ 19 ❧

The doorbell rang as Josie was busy picking up stray toys and straightening out magazines. "Are you Josephine Bain?" A casually dressed, balding, middle-aged man about Josie's height greeted her as she opened the door. Behind him, a new, oversized luxury car was parked in the driveway next to Josie's dented, six-year-old minivan.

"Yes I'm Josie, you must be Dr. Stokes. Please come in." Josie stood aside to welcome him. Her light brown hair was freshly dyed and highlighted to cover the gray and her face was lightly made up. She smiled and showed the custody evaluator into her scrubbed and polished kitchen.

Austen rode around the house on his tricycle, freshly bathed, with his hair combed and his new outfit still clean. "Phoebe's in school." Josie said, and offered the evaluator a cup of coffee.

"Yes, I know. I'll interview her at my office next week," Dr. Stokes said matter-of-factly. "I'm here to observe you, Mrs. Bain. I want to see your parenting style with Austen."

"Okay, that's fine, Dr. Stokes. Well, on mornings when Phoebe's in school we're not usually home. We go the park or the library or visit my mom. I do errands in the morning. Then we usually come home for lunch and after that Austen takes a nap."

Suddenly Austen crashed his tricycle into the wall, inches from Dr. Stokes's leg. He looked up at the strange man and said "my Mommy is very mean!" Then he pedaled backwards a few feet before crashing into the wall again, for good measure. "She's very mean!" The little boy said sternly. Josie glanced nervously at Dr. Stokes and thought she detected a faint smile on the evaluator's face.

"I have no idea why he would say that, Dr. Stokes." Josie laughed nervously and crouched down talk to Austen. "Austen, really! You know I'm not mean!" She stood up. "I pretty much let him do what he wants as long as it's not dangerous. He rides in the house as long as the gate at the top of the stairs is closed," she said, walking over to demonstrate the sturdy safety gate.

"We read and play games. We're both artistic so I have a little studio set up and Austen has his paints on a table right next to mine. Here I can show you." Josie led the evaluator into a spare bedroom.

"It's really pretty boring here for the most part, Dr. Stokes. My life is pretty tame. We watch kid movies and go to little league games. I bake cookies. I'm kind of ordinary."

Josie took him into each of the kid's rooms and out into the garden. He glanced around Phoebe's purple bedroom lined with dolls and looked in her closet full of clothes. He watched as Josie took the cookies she'd baked off the cooling rack and gave one to Austen. All the while he silently took notes, without so much as a nod. After about an hour he left and told Josie he would be in touch.

"I felt like a lab rat." Josie sat on the back steps and kicked off her shoes while Austen played in the grass. She'd phoned Alice as soon as the evaluator pulled out of the driveway. "He just followed me around and took notes and didn't say anything. Austen went up to him right away and said 'my Mommy is mean' – can you believe it? I am so not mean."

"So you and Richard paid fifteen thousand for this? What a racket. What happens next?" Alice asked.

"We both have to take a psychological test and then I have to bring Phoebe in for an interview. According to the lawyer, the restraining order is being lifted next week, but Richard can't be alone with the kids. He has to have someone else there – a family member most likely. Anyway, he has to do the same thing I just did – have Dr. Stokes follow him around his house for a couple hours while he takes care of the kids. Of course he'll be on his extra good behavior. Not the usual yelling - screaming - hitting and crying scenario."

"Hey Josie, just a thought, what if I came out next week for a mini vacation? We can take the kids to Fisherman's Wharf or something," Alice suggested.

"You're welcome here anytime Alice. There's plenty of room. I can probably pick you up at the airport. I'd love to have some company. More and more I avoid talking to my other friends and neighbors because this divorce is taking over my life and I don't really have anything else to talk about right now. I know it's not something most people want to talk about. If you haven't been through it you just don't get it. Anyway, it would be great to hang out for a few days." Josie smiled to herself as she watched Austen play with the dog.

"Okay, I'll call as soon as I book the ticket. Tim said he'd take care of my dogs for a few days." Alice said goodbye and hung up.

❧ 20 ❧

Josie waited on a narrow bench outside the courtroom while her attorney went inside to speak to the clerk. A little girl in a frilly pink dress twirled around the dimly lit hallway while her parents spoke to their adoption attorney. Wendy Pepper came out of the courtroom holding a thin manila folder.

"Here's the transcript. This is the court's copy. They're letting us have five minutes to look it over. There's an attorney from Weiner's office waiting to look at it next. We're not allowed to make copies so try to remember everything you can." Wendy sat down next to her client and took the stapled document out of the folder.

"How are we supposed to be able to read this?" Josie asked glancing through the pages. "The whole thing is almost completely blacked out."

"Yes, it's heavily redacted," Wendy agreed. "They have to do that to protect the privacy of the people mentioned in the report." Wendy flipped through the few sheets of paper. "Well, we took a gamble and we lost. It wasn't worth the attorney fees it cost you to get this thing. We can't use it." Wendy shrugged and put the papers back in the folder. She went back into the courtroom and handed the folder to an attorney from Weiner's office, a tall man in his early thirties with a sour expression. Josie watched as Wendy walked over to talk to the court clerk while the other attorney sat down with the papers on his lap and quickly took photos of all the pages with his cell phone.

After seeing the useless, heavily redacted document, Josie drove straight to the CPS office. She sat in her car for several minutes, trying to compose herself. She'd been warned by her attorney never to talk to Phoebe about the abuse she'd suffered from Richard and never to ask her about the CPS interview. Her attorney emphasized that if the court or the evaluator ever found out she'd discussed any of these subjects with Phoebe she would be accused of manipulating her daughter and fabricating the abuse.

Now she was upset. It wasn't just that the social worker had told her to split from Richard under threat of losing her children, it was also that she was being prevented from even knowing what her seven-year-old had said in the interview, and most importantly being able to use it in court to counter Richard's lies.

"I need to speak to Ms. Grimes," Josie said to the clerk in the CPS office. "Have a seat and I'll have Ms. Grimes call you shortly." Josie impatiently scanned through her phone as she waited to be called.

A few minutes later the clerk called her name. "I'm sorry Mrs. Bain; Ms. Grimes can't see you now. Your case is closed and her report has been filed. Do you have something new to report?"

Josie leaned into the window. "No, I just need to talk to her. I don't understand what she did. I just need to talk to her. I want to understand. The entire transcript of her interview with my daughter was blacked out. My attorney said it was to protect people. Protect who? I need to know! I demand to know! My ex-husband's attorney is claiming that I fabricated the entire thing! Everything is being twisted to make me look bad!" Josie raised her voice as she glanced around the empty room.

"She told me I had to leave my marriage or she could take away my children! Then she threw me under the bus! Her report said basically nothing happened after all! And I spent money on my attorney to get a copy of the transcript and it was all blacked out! Something is wrong! I demand to talk to her!" The clerk got up and left her window while Josie was ranting. Turning around, Josie saw a security guard walking up behind her.

"You'll have to leave now, ma'am," the guard told her as he guided her by the elbow. He handed her a card with the La Costa County insignia on it. "You can direct all your complaints here – this is the address and phone number." Josie took the card, tore it in half, and threw it on the ground as she left the building. She scowled at the security guard as she stormed off, threw her purse in her car, and started the engine.

∽ 21 ∾

Josie peered through the lens of the dusty microfilm machine in the back corner of the main county library as she scanned through decades-old copies of the San Francisco newspaper. Austen was in the children's section listening to story time with Valerie, and Josie had another twenty minutes to try to find what she was looking for.

Richard had a way of deflecting any questions about his family on the few occasions when she asked him. She assumed he was a typical guy and didn't really pay attention to family history. Richard's father had been dead for many years and the family had built him up into an almost mythical figure. He was a man with a sixth grade education who went on to become the chief building inspector in San Francisco. He came from poverty but died a multi-millionaire.

Something didn't add up though, because Richard's father spent his entire career working for the city and had never made that much money. Certainly not enough to amass the fortune that the family laid claim to. After Richard's father died, his father's best friend, Phil, had been criminally prosecuted for his role in a scandal involving the building inspection department. Now that Richard was spending his father's money to destroy her, and his father's old friend Phil had deliberately lied to the court in order to make her look bad, it was imperative for Josie to find out the truth about Richard's family. And the truth lay somewhere in those strands of microfilm.

Josie raced through the reams of data, her eyes trained to stop at anything that mentioned the FBI or the building inspection department. Then she saw it. She stopped the machine and flipped back through an old department store advertisement. There it was. Bingo. Richard's father, along with several other men, had been named in an FBI indictment over twenty years earlier. She quickly printed the article and raced back to the children's section to meet up with her mother and son.

"Mom, look at this," Josie whispered to Valerie as the librarian read the last few pages of the children's book. Austen sat cross-legged in a circle with several other small children.

"What is it?" Valerie took the sheet. "Wow. He was indicted on corruption charges. This is amazing, Josie." Valerie glanced through the article.

"You know there has to be a lot more to the story," Josie whispered. "I'd like to do some more digging – I know I can't use it in my case but I really need to know the truth about the family I married into." Story time ended and Austen ran off to play. Valerie and Josie followed him and discussed the article. "I'd like to know what came of it – was there a trial? Was he convicted of anything?" Josie wondered.

"Or maybe he had a good attorney and got off just like his buddy Phil," Valerie added.

"My attorney told me to keep writing so I'm going to slip something in about how Richard can spend thousands on his attorney to destroy me in court because of his father's ill-gotten gains."

"Well, I think when you have time you should try to find out more – not because it will make a difference in your case because I don't think it will. You need to know because it's always important to know the truth. You need to know what you're dealing with." Valerie shivered. "Richard and his family are ethically and morally bankrupt. This is one more reason why you need to get primary custody – God forbid he teaches Austen and Phoebe to behave like him."

"I know, Mom. I want my kids to know that it does matter what you do and how you behave, regardless of whether anyone else can prove it," Josie agreed.

❦ 22 ❦

Josie nosed her car up to the airport curb as Alice rushed over with her luggage. "The back is unlocked, just throw your bag in," Josie yelled out the open window. Alice tossed her luggage in the back and climbed into the front seat.

"How are you guys?" Alice turned to greet Phoebe and Austen, who were strapped into their car seats in the back.

"We're fine, Alice. We can't wait to show what we got for Christmas!" Phoebe replied, hugging the back of Alice's seat.

"Okay kids. Is everyone strapped in? I need to get back on the freeway before the traffic gets any worse." Josie pulled away from the curb. "How was the flight? It's been a while! It's so good to see you!" Josie smiled at her old friend.

"We're going to have a good time kids!" Alice took her snow hat off and flipped open the mirror on the visor to check her hair. "Your mom and I have a bunch of stuff planned! We're taking you guys to the city and the zoo and to that ice cream place – what's that place we went to that time, Josie? The place with the huge banana splits?"

Alice glanced out the window at the traffic as Josie merged onto the freeway. "Oh, the flight was fine. I hate flying but I'm getting too old for those all-night road trips," Alice said, settling into her seat.

"I have so much stuff to tell you. I can't really talk in front of the kids but when we get back I'll put them to bed and we can stay up with a glass of wine. I'll put a fire in my faux fire place." Josie laughed. "I'm finding out so much stuff I never knew. It just keeps getting curiouser and curiouser, as they say. Pretty much nothing is the way I thought it was." Josie glanced into her rear view mirror and saw Austen slumped over, asleep in his car seat. She glanced over her shoulder and saw Phoebe, still awake, looking out her window.

"I get that you're trying not to get in trouble with the court Josie, but I hope no one ever tries to tell me what I can and can't say in the privacy of my own home or car. Jesus! What about the First Amendment?" Alice whispered to her friend.

"I know. I hate it too. But like I said, nothing is the way I thought it was. I'm through the looking glass now and I've come out on the other side into a world that I don't even recognize. We can talk later." They drove in silence out of the city, through the tunnel and down the winding tree-lined road to Josie's suburban house.

"I think I may finally have the goods on Richard's family," Josie said as she handed Alice a glass of the cabernet she'd been saving for a special occasion. "Not that it matters. It's not like it will change anything in court. It's more about my need to understand how I got here and why Richard did what he did." The kids were in bed and Josie sat down in the chair opposite the couch.

"So what did you find out?" Alice sat on the couch with her feet up and took a sip of wine.

"His father was indicted along with several other people from the San Francisco building department. Apparently they had a scam where they would 'red tag' a building and then buy it from the victim for pennies on the dollar. They convinced the victim that the building was basically worthless. The victims were mostly immigrants who spoke little or no English and had no clue. Then the property was deeded to various people – I went through some of the records at city hall for one of the properties – it was an apartment building in Noe Valley – it was a tangled mess of deeds and quit claims and various names of bogus companies. They were very careful to hide what they were doing. It would take days to sort out even one property. But the gist of it was that Richard's dad and his friends were ripping off property and deeding it among some sham companies they set up while they 'cleared' the phony building code violations that they'd fabricated to rip off the original owners. Eventually they'd sell the buildings and split the proceeds. I have no idea how the FBI got on to it, but, let's face it, the owners couldn't have been stupid - they must have known they were ripped off, even if they didn't understand exactly what was happening. I remember Richard told me that his dad always carried a weapon - supposedly to protect himself from crooked contractors. In reality, he was probably afraid of the building owners he'd screwed over. Anyway, it went on for years. There was more stuff, too. Apparently there were also bribes from contractors and other stuff."

"Wow, Josie. That could be a movie or something. What about your mother-in-law? Do you think she knew about it?" Alice took another sip of her wine.

"Of course she knew. How else does an uneducated city worker end up living in Hillsborough and putting his daughter through Harvard? She knew and looked the other way. Like any good mafia wife."

"God Josie, you married the mob."

"Maybe not the mob, but now I know Richard has criminality in his family background. The only problem is that apparently his dad never stood trial – it looks like they may have cut a deal with him. In any case, his dad retired right after the indictments came down and then he ended up getting cancer. He died about a year later. Richard has never even told me exactly when his dad died much less anything about the indictment." Josie got up and handed Alice a copy of the twenty-year-old newspaper article.

"I agree you can't directly use it in court, Josie. Even though we know that Richard has the same criminal mindset that his father had, you can't blame the child for the sins of the parent. However…" Alice paused and said with emphasis "you can work this into a declaration for the custody evaluator as one more reason not to even think about giving him custody. You know he'll be teaching the same slimy tricks to your kids as soon as he has a chance. The fruit never falls far from the tree."

"Don't say that, Alice. When it comes to my kids, the fruit isn't going to fall anywhere near the Bain family tree. In fact, now that I understand what this family is all about, I have even more reason to take the kids to Montana."

"What does the lawyer say about that? Tim said it would be almost impossible in most situations to get a judge to let you take the kids out of state," Alice said.

"I have an early hearing tomorrow so I'll ask the attorney about it then. I plan to drop Phoebe off at school early and you can hang out with Austen until I get back."

 23

Weiner and Richard were huddled at the end of the hallway while Josie paced nervously outside the courtroom. It was less than five minutes until her hearing and Wendy wasn't there. The bailiff opened the courtroom door and people started filing in. Josie took a seat in the back and turned off her phone. Just as the bailiff was calling for everyone to rise, Wendy appeared.

"Cutting it a little close there aren't you, Pepper?" Weiner said with a smirk as Wendy walked in the courtroom. "Hey, if it isn't my old friend Adam Weiner – well just look at you! You clean up real good! Who'd have thought it? But you might want to double check your comb-over." Wendy shot back at Weiner as she nudged Josie to move down a seat. She was dressed in a business suit and pulled a bulging wheeled brief case behind her.

"I'm always here – you can count on me – even if I'm not on time." She whispered to Josie. "They do this alphabetically anyway – the hearing starts at eight but they call the cases in alphabetical order."

"Yes, I already figured that out but my last name is Bain," Josie whispered back sharply.

"Are the parties present for the Bain matter?" The bailiff called out. Weiner stood up. "Adam Weiner here, representing Richard Bain, who is also present."

"Wendy Pepper here, representing Mrs. Bain." Wendy stood up and walked towards the front of the courtroom. Richard sat down next to his attorney and Josie followed Wendy to the opposite table.

"I've read your filing and I've issued a preliminary ruling Ms. Pepper. Are you going to make an oral argument?" The judge was tall and thin with glasses perched on his angular face.

Wendy spoke loudly and without a trace of nervousness. "Your Honor, the marital home is the major community asset. It is our position that the housing market has peaked, and my client wants the house to be sold or have the other party buy out her share, immediately. Waiting to sell will unfairly disadvantage my client. She needs the proceeds from the house to start over somewhere else. I petition the court to allow her to sell the house and put the proceeds into escrow pending the final settlement. I have attached two proposals from local real estate agents to my motion as well as evidence that my client has readied the house for sale at her expense. I have also attached expert opinions regarding the forecast for the housing market." Wendy stopped talking and looked over at Weiner.

Weiner cleared his throat and began to speak. "Your Honor, my client wants the marital home and will buy his wife's share at the time of the settlement. He needs time to come up with the money and will do so as part of a global settlement agreement. Your Honor, my client doesn't feel it's fair to ask both parties to pay the cost of the sale when it is his intention to continue owning the house."

"I deny Mrs. Bain's motion to sell the marital house. Mr. Bain should not have to bear his half of the costs of selling since he wants to continue owning the house." The judge banged his gavel.

Wendy looked over at Josie and shrugged. She stuffed some papers back into her brief case and followed Weiner and Richard out of the courtroom.

"That's it? Motion denied? What am I supposed to do now? Wait for Richard to buy me out? The newspaper is already talking about the housing market softening."

Wendy glanced at her client and kept walking. "Listen, I have another hearing in fifteen minutes. I'll call when I get back to the office. We need to get an agreement about when he's going to buy you out."

Wendy wasn't surprised at the ruling. She'd been making her living in this courthouse for over a decade and her father had practiced family law there for three decades before her. She knew the judge. He and Weiner played doubles tennis with their wives every weekend. As long as they didn't discuss particular cases it was business as usual. She'd also been to a Bar association event in the wine country a few months earlier which had been underwritten by Weiner's law firm. She'd seen the judge and his wife there, along with Weiner and other members of his firm, all dining at the same table. It was all just business as usual in the La Costa County family court.

24

Alice pushed Austen in his jogging stroller as she and Josie hiked around the reservoir. "I understand how this happened. It happened because I married someone I didn't really know and I made assumptions about him I shouldn't have made." Josie was slightly out of breath trying to keep up with her more athletic friend.

"I understand why it happened as far as Richard being from the type of family he's from and how the family got ahead in life by basically stealing other people's property. I just can't get over the fact that we really had it made. We have two great kids. We live in one of the best neighborhoods. We had a good income. I just can't seem to get past what a total waste it all is."

"He's just an angry guy, Josie. The world is full of them. He's almost fifty and he's disappointed in his life. He's angry. He took his anger out on you and the kids. He probably doesn't even really understand it himself. It's not like he's an introspective guy. Anyway, every decent woman I've ever met has at least one crappy marriage under her belt.

Just move forward. Try not to look back." Alice was never one to over analyze a situation.

"I'm more worried about your future, Josie. Forget the past. It's over and you can't change it. I noticed you got something from the lawyer," Alice said.

"It was a bill. Just one more bill I can't pay. I've gone through the money my mom gave me. I canceled the newspaper and the cable TV first thing. I bought paint and cleaning supplies to get the house ready for sale – only to find out I'm not allowed to sell it. We never eat out. I put the fees for the evaluator on my credit card. With the rental income and the temporary family support from Richard we can barely pay the mortgage and utilities. I'm going into some serious debt every month not even counting the attorney fees. I really need to get that move-away." They were back in the parking lot and Josie folded up the stroller while Alice strapped Austen into his car seat.

"I was afraid this was going to happen," Alice said. "Can't you see? Richard has a massive war chest to spend on lawyers. They'll just bury you in paperwork and wait you out. They can afford to. Quite frankly I'm not impressed by that attorney you hired. Tim and I both think you can do a better job by yourself."

"I can't, Alice. I wouldn't know the first thing about it. I'm an engineer. I do things that make sense. I solve problems. I am lost in this family court system. Nothing makes any sense. My attorney mentioned something to me about Weiner and the judge being friends. What the heck it that about? How does that work? I thought that wasn't supposed to happen. I thought judges weren't supposed to be friends with the attorneys that appear before them. Isn't that a conflict of interest or something?"

"It's like any work place, Josie. You get to know the people you work with. Weiner and the judge belong to the same bar association. They socialize in the same circles. They might have even been classmates in law school. Where do you think these judges come from anyway? They mostly come from the same group of lowlife divorce attorneys. Don't be so naïve, Josie."

"I don't think I'm that naïve." Josie said as she started the car. "I bet most people are naïve about this stuff. I don't think most people know that judges can be tennis partners with attorneys that appear in their courtroom and it's considered hunky dory. How do I know they didn't talk about our case? How do I know he doesn't just automatically rule in favor of Weiner just because they're friends?"

"You don't, of course. In fact you can probably assume that they do talk and it isn't fair. Weiner is a high-dollar attorney. Why do you think he gets paid so much? Are his courtroom skills really that impressive? I saw Richard's financial disclosure - he's already paid Weiner almost twice what you've paid your attorney," Alice paused.

"Here's how it works, Josie. You get as much justice as you can afford to pay for. Richard can afford a lot more than you. When there are two wealthy people getting divorced, the game is to go around town and put retainers in at all the high-dollar firms so your spouse is stuck with a crap attorney who doesn't play tennis with the judge. Pay to play, Josie. Them's the facts," Alice said with a flourish.

"Leaving your job was the biggest mistake you could have made," Alice continued. "It gave Richard all the leverage in the relationship. He knew your family couldn't help you much and your paycheck and support system from your work was gone. The coup de grace was hiding your license renewal notice. He probably knew that losing your license and having to take a rigorous exam after just having had a baby was too much for you. Richard also knew he had acquired a significant claim to your property because you put the money in your joint account. He had you coming and going, Josie." Alice realized she'd upset her friend. "I'm sorry, Josic. It's in the past. It's not your fault.

"I know. I beat myself up about that stuff all the time," Josie said. "Hindsight is twenty-twenty and all that. Anyway, tell me something I don't already know." Josie shrugged.

∽ 25 ∽

"So why did Richard's dad and his dad's co-workers do that? I mean, they did it for money obviously but why else - was it just pure greed?" Alice said, reaching into the fridge for a half-finished bottle of wine.

"Of course, it was pure greed. They did it because they could. They had the power and they abused it. Corruption. Abuse of power. That's what the FBI got them on. It probably started gradually, and then they went too far like people do. It's greed that drove them, though." Josie pounded a lump of dough with her flour-covered fist.

"The whole department was mostly white guys when Richard worked there years later, so you know it was probably all white guys when Richard's father was the head of it. In other words, they weren't ripping off people like themselves. They targeted foreigners and non-whites."

"Phil was indicted separately by the city attorney," Josie continued. "He wasn't part of the corruption investigation. In fact, he never worked for the city. Phil's father was a judge, and somehow Phil became a San Francisco real estate mogul. I guess he knew how the system worked and was somehow part of the building department scheme. I still haven't figured out all the details and it doesn't really matter now, anyway." Josie rolled out the dough while Alice poured two glasses of wine.

"People can justify anything. Richard is so proud to be a native San Franciscan and his family makes snarky comments about people who come here from somewhere else. So maybe it was just the fact that the victims were mostly foreigners and that made them fair game." Josie took four plates out of the cupboard and put them on the table, before going into the living room and turning off the TV.

"Dinner time kids – please wash your hands," she called out.

"Mom, can we eat in the living room tonight? Please?" Phoebe begged.

"Well, okay. I guess the pizza isn't too messy. Just make sure the dog doesn't grab Austen's dinner okay?" Josie agreed, as the kids ran to get their pizza.

"I don't know what the arrangement was, but my mother-in-law has an income which is far more than she'd get from a city pension from twenty years ago," Josie said, as she cut up her pizza. "My guess is there's still some sort of payoff going on. When Richard and I were planning our wedding Phil offered to pay for the reception. Ten thousand bucks! When I thanked him he told me that he'd made a promise to Richard's father on his death bed that he'd always look out for Richard." Josie continued to eat her pizza. "You know what I think?"

"What?" Alice asked.

"I think Richard's dad told Richard all the dirty little details of the scam – basically where all the bodies are buried – and may have even given Richard some documents that could be used against Phil if needed. You know there's no honor among thieves. I mean, why else would Phil show up in Richard's hour of need time and again? Why else would he pay for the wedding reception and perjure himself in court for Richard? What's in it for him?" Josie continued.

"My mother-in-law also has a couple of small apartment buildings in the city. My sister-in-law lives in one with her husband, and Richard's cousins live in the other. A couple of the apartments have been vacant for years. One thing Richard always said was that his family never sells property."

"Why wouldn't they ever sell property?" Alice asked.

"I don't know," Josie said as she got up to check on the kids. "Maybe they know the father's scam was a one-time thing, and they're lucky he died before he ended up convicted. I mean, if you knew you had valuable stolen property maybe you'd hang on to it forever, too. Maybe they don't want some title company doing a title search that could open up a can of worms." Josie shrugged.

"Wow, what a pile of manure. Good thing you're getting out of that family," Alice said quietly. "At the end of the day you have a huge advantage over him, because you know how to take care of yourself. You don't need to grab things that don't belong to you and hold on to them for dear life for fear someone somewhere might find out. I still believe that in the end, crime doesn't pay." Alice took a bite of pizza.

"It's not fair that he has all this money to use against you Josie, but life isn't fair. You just have to play the cards you've been dealt. Forget about hanging on to the house. You may need to fight just to hang on to what you had when you met him. Just protect the kids, and don't look back. The future is wide open and you need to jump in and create a better life for them. I've seen you do it before and I know you can do it again. Live and learn," Alice said.

26

Josie stood in front of her living room windows and looked down at the scene below. Richard had pulled his car to the top of the driveway, and Andrew had pulled up beside him, blocking the garage. The two men talked for a few minutes before approaching the house.

"Phoebe and Austen, Dad's here to pick you up." Josie rolled their suitcase to the top of the stairs.

"Mommy, I don't want to go." Phoebe walked into the kitchen carrying her brother.

"Please put Austen down, Phoebe. You have to go, sweetie. Daddy is allowed to see you guys now. Someone else will be with you all the time. It looks like Andrew will be with you. I'm sure they have something fun planned." Austen squirmed free of his sister and ran to his mother.

"It's going to be fine, Austen. You're going to spend the night with Daddy. I'll be right here at home waiting for you," Josie crouched down and put her hand on Austen's face.

"Don't want to go. Daddy scary." Austen's eyes filled with tears. Josie wrapped her arms around him.

"I've planned a special treat for when you guys get back tomorrow. But you won't get it unless you're good and you go with Daddy. Everything will be fine. Daddy has another grown-up with him all the time when he is with you guys." The dog ran to the door barking, just as the bell rang.

Josie took a deep breath before opening the door. She stepped back quickly as Richard brusquely pushed his way into the house. Andrew sneered at her as he followed his cousin up the stairs.

"How are my kids?" Richard said in a booming voice as he uncharacteristically bent down to hug the children. Phoebe had her arms around Austen and warily took a step away from her father. "I missed you so much!" Richard said as he wiped tears from his eyes.

Oh my God. He opens the spigot and the crocodile tears start gushing out. Jesus. He manufactures phony tears as easily as snapping his fingers. Give me a break, Josie thought to herself, shaking her head in disbelief at the waterworks show Richard was putting on.

Andrew took Phoebe by the hand and hurried her down the stairs. Phoebe reached out to Josie as she was hastily swept past and put into the back of Andrew's car. Meanwhile, Richard picked up his sullen and reluctant son. Austen started to cry and reached for Josie as his father carried him out of the house. Josie felt a lump in her throat as she watched. After putting Austen in his car, Richard walked back to the house where Josie stood in the doorway.

"Don't forget this, Richard," Josie said as she handed him the suitcase. Richard leaned over to pick it up and muttered to her under his breath.

"This morning my sister asked me if there was some way we could just have you killed." He glared at his wife.

"Wow, Richard, you just had your restraining order lifted and you come over here and threaten me? This is unbelievable. Telling me that your sister wants me killed is just as much a threat as you telling me you want me killed. Maybe I need to go back to court and get another restraining order against you." Josie quickly shut the door as Richard picked up the suitcase and left.

A few minutes later, Alice returned from her morning run and was cooling off on the front porch. Josie sat down beside her, carrying a cup of coffee.

"Richard just left with the kids. He had Andrew with him. And he was driving a brand new car. Some kind of fancy SUV," Josie said. Alice looked at her, surprised.

"Geez, Josie, if I'd known he was coming I would have stayed here with you." Alice leaned back on her elbows.

"I know. I guess I should have mentioned it. Now that the kids aren't here we can talk more freely, though." Josie deliberately hadn't told Alice about the morning pick-up because she wasn't sure what Alice would do.

"Richard said his sister wants to get me killed," Josie said blandly. "As if."

Alice looked at her friend with a startled expression. "Wow, what an asshole. Of course, since you were alone you don't have any witnesses that he said that. Too bad, that's an obvious threat. I didn't want to say anything earlier, but Tim and I have been worried about you, Josie. There's so much at stake. And the more I hear about Richard and his family... well I can't put anything past him."

"I'm not worried about it." Josie stood up to go in the house. "I don't put anything past him either – but these days it's pretty hard to get someone killed without getting caught - especially in the middle of an ugly divorce."

The two women entered the house and walked into the kitchen. "I don't doubt Richard's father and his cohorts were capable of anything, but it was easier to get away with stuff back then. Don't forget the Bain family motto: 'You can't prove it.' They wouldn't have any qualms about killing the mother of Austen and Phoebe; except that there's a good chance someone would be able to prove it."

"Well at least document that he said that to you," Alice said. "I'm not surprised he got a new car. I've been checking his social media. It looks like he's dating some woman he met through his sister. He'll get remarried. Those kinds of guys always do. Yuck." Alice grabbed a towel from the linen closet and went into the hall bathroom to shower.

꩜ 27 ꩜

"Are the parties present for the Bain matter?" The bailiff scanned the gallery. It had been several months since Josie's custody evaluation, and Dr. Stokes had finally issued his report.

"Yes, Your Honor." Weiner and Richard stood up. "Adam Weiner representing Mr. Bain. Mr. Bain is present." Richard sheepishly followed his attorney through the swinging gate of the courtroom barrier, and sat down at the petitioner's table, as Josie and Wendy sat down at the respondent's table.

"We're here to discuss the recommendations of the custody evaluator," the judge said, as he flipped through the thirty-page, fifteen-thousand-dollar report.

When Josie had finally seen the typo-ridden report she was shocked. "For five hundred dollars per page, he could at least have paid an editor," she'd told her mother. It didn't surprise her that Richard hadn't done much to impress the evaluator, but it upset her that the evaluator didn't seem to hold it against him much either. In her mind, the content of the report was just as flawed as the presentation.

Dr. Stokes reported that Richard had deliberately tried to ditch him on a winding country road when they were driving separate cars to take the kids hiking during his observation day. Richard's psychological testing had revealed his narcissistic personality disorder. The evaluator also noted that, while Richard claimed to have taken the court-ordered parenting class, he'd never actually provided any proof, as was required.

On the other hand, Stokes had pronounced Josie to be an 'excellent parent,' and despite Weiner's attempt to slander her in court by declaring that she had psychological problems because she'd seen a therapist in the past, the psychological testing had not revealed any abnormal traits or syndromes on her part.

Reading through the report, it became clear to both Josie and her attorney that she'd knocked it out of the park. From what Josie could tell, she deserved an A+ and Richard deserved an F. Then she got to the final section where Dr. Stokes put forth his recommendations. He made it very clear that he was reluctantly agreeing to allow Josie to move to Montana with the kids. Josie felt like she'd been kicked in the stomach. The evaluator had basically given her a B- and he'd given Richard a C+.

When she was preparing for the evaluation, Josie had read Dr. Stokes's book, along with all the articles she could find that he'd authored. In his book, Dr. Stokes made his bias very clear: Osama bin laden doesn't get married to Joan of Arc, as he put it. Dr. Stokes wrote that if one half of the couple was disreputable, then it was safe to assume that they both were. His blatant bias was especially shocking to Josie because Dr. Stokes was considered a leader in his field.

After stating that Josie could move to Montana with the kids, the evaluator set out a complicated visitation schedule which meant that the children would be flying back-and-forth to California five times per year, and that Richard would be flying to Montana several times per year. Richard was going to spend far more time with Phoebe and Austen after the divorce than he ever did during the marriage. When Josie read that Dr. Stokes had given Richard all the major holidays, along with most of the summer and every single spring break, Josie felt like she'd been stabbed through the heart. She was getting the move-away but she was paying dearly for it.

"We accept the report and ask that it be adopted as an order of the court," Wendy told the judge forthrightly. Wendy was frankly surprised when she read the report, and was doubly surprised that her client was upset about it. Josie failed to appreciate what she'd accomplished. She'd been granted a move-away. This was the first time in Wendy's experience that a court-ordered evaluator had granted an out-of-state move to one of the parties. All she could think was that Weiner's client had totally bombed. She tried to impress on Josie that nothing else mattered. She'd gotten her move-away and now she basically needed to shut up.

"Does the petitioner concur?" The judge asked.

"We do, Your Honor. We also request that the case be bifurcated, so that my client can remarry," Weiner said. "The property settlement has dragged on for months and he needs to move on with his life."

"We object, Your Honor. The court denied our motion to sell the marital home and it continues to lose value months later. Petitioner stalls and delays the buyout, and cancels settlement meetings at the last minute. This is a ploy on the part of petitioner to buy my client out months or years into the future as the housing market contin-ues to decline. My client also wants to move on with her life, Your Honor, and to do so she needs her share of the marital property," Wendy concluded.

The judge hesitated a moment and looked at Josie. "Motion to bifurcate the divorce is granted," he suddenly announced. "The divorce will be effective at the end of the year, and the parties are free to remarry. The property distribution will be set for trial if the parties don't come to terms." The judge banged his gavel.

Wendy looked at Josie and shrugged. "Let's talk outside." Josie followed her out of the courtroom.

"What does this mean?" Josie whispered to her attorney, as Richard and Weiner walked by with smirks on their faces.

"As far as your case is concerned, it means he's going to continue stalling as long as the housing market is going down. When it starts to look like the market is picking up, he'll finally settle. It means you won't be getting the money you would have gotten if we'd been able to list the house like we wanted. Sorry Josie. You got your move-away. Except for the property settlement the divorce will be final at the end of the year. You can take the kids and move the next day if you want. Trust me; they aren't happy with the report. Weiner never thought you'd get a move-away. You win some, you lose some." Wendy shrugged again and walked down the hall.

Josie followed. "I know you're busy, but I have to talk to you." Wendy paused and looked at her client. "You advised me to accept the report so I did. But after I move I never get to have Christmas with my kids again. I never get to have Thanksgiving with them. I'm the parent who packs the lunches and drives them to their activities. I only get them for two weeks in the summer and no spring break ever! How is that fair?" Josie raised her voice.

"You got a move-away. Nobody in this courthouse gets a move-away. Do you understand? As far as the other stuff, nothing is carved in stone. I told you that already. After you get settled in Montana, we can file another motion to revise the visitation. So, is that all? I'm already late..." Wendy glanced nervously down the hallway.

"There's one more thing..."

Wendy tapped her foot impatiently as she waited for Josie to continue.

"There isn't going to be another motion. I've spent all the money I have and I've tapped out all my credit cards," Josie said.

"Well then," Wendy paused. "I'm sorry to hear that. I'll have my secretary send you a substitution of attorney. Sign it and send it back, and I'll get it on the docket. You'll be listed on the docket as pro-per. That means you'll have to represent yourself."

Wendy shook Josie's hand before rushing to her next case. She'd been expecting this and was frankly surprised that Josie had kept up with her payments as well as she had. Each time she'd filed a motion for Josie, she'd asked for a modest amount of attorney fees and as expected, the requests were always denied. In Wendy's experience, even when there was a large disparity in income between the parties, attorney fee awards were seldom granted to the lower income party.

When she was a young attorney working for her father, he'd explained the dirty little secret about attorney fee awards: basically, they were bad for business. If the Richard Bains of the world knew they would be required to pay the attorney fees for the other side in order to level the playing field, the result would be a drastic decline in litigation. As much as the people who work in the family court system love to complain about excessive litigation, it was their life blood and they weren't about to do anything to jeopardize it. If the motion to sell the marital home had been successful, or if the judge had awarded attorney fees to Josie, things would be different. As it was, the money was gone, and Wendy was relieved to be done with the case.

Josie tossed her notebook in the car and swallowed two migraine pills before crawling into the back seat. Lying on her side, she draped her jacket over her body, and covered her throbbing head with her arms as she pressed her eyes shut. After three nights of insomnia leading up to the custody hearing, she fell into a restless sleep.

The bear was huge, over nine feet tall on his hind legs. His golden brown coat glistened in the afternoon sun. He had the distinctive curved ski-slope nose of the North American Brown Bear – also known as the Grizzly. Josie followed from a short distance as he lumbered down the mountain path. They were walking on a sacred trail carved into the side of the mountain, three thousand feet above a rocky, river canyon.

"Always take the high road," the bear said. "It is more defensible." After a short time they stopped on a rock outcropping, overlooking the canyon. Josie looked out at the sweeping and unrestricted view. In the canyon far below were several men with hunting rifles. Some were clambering over rocks, while others were standing together looking down river or gazing up at the mountains looming before them.

"The enemy takes the low road. They are many and you are few." Josie listened to the bear's comment, as she cupped her hands over her eyes to block the sun. She could make out Richard and Weiner, along with what looked like several other Bain family members, and a couple of Richard's friends.

"I have no weapon," Josie told the bear. "How am I to defend myself?" The bear stood a few feet away and gazed down at the canyon, saying nothing. Josie sat cross legged on the warm rock. She looked to her side and there was a bow and arrow.

She picked up the bow and arrow and stood. Carefully placing the arrow on the bow string, she drew it back as far as she could. Bracing herself, with her knees slightly bent, she focused on the men in the canyon below, looking for a target. Richard's primary weapon against her was his family's money. With that money, he was able to pay a mercenary to fight his unprovoked war. Josie decided that her target was Weiner.

She took aim at the attorney who was busy pointing to something up river, unaware of the danger he was in. Josie exhaled slowly and completely to still her body, just as her father had taught her during shooting practice growing up in Montana. She was known for her steady hand, and her sharp vision. As she slowly exhaled, she released her only arrow into the canyon below.

A lone arrow flew from her bow, and Josie watched in amazement as millions of arrows magically filled the sky, raining destruction on the men below.

"Your words are your weapons," the bear said to Josie, before turning to walk away.

"Wait," Josie called after him. "Is that all?"

The bear continued down the path. Without looking back her said, "speak the truth and your words will be fiercer than all of their rifles."

❦ 28 ❧

"Pepper said I can only take personal belongings like clothing and books, and toys for the kids. We can leave as soon as New Year's Day." Josie sat on a park bench next to her mother watching Austen climb onto a play structure amid the brilliant colors of late autumn.

"Are you sure you want to move to Montana on New Year's? Why move in the winter?" Valerie asked her daughter.

"Because I have to, Mother. I'm going broke trying to pay the mortgage here. Besides, I like winter in Montana. It's not like the Sierras. The snow is dry and powdery – remember? The kids will love it. I'll take them to the ski hill. We'll build snowmen in the yard. And it's so beautiful and quiet when it's snowing outside and there's a fire in the fireplace." Josie reminisced about her former home town.

"Alice will meet us at the airport and we can stay with her for a few days. The property manager has a two bedroom apartment coming up in December – I told him to hold it for me. What I really need to know is can you come up there with us?" Josie turned to her mother.

"I'm seventy-six years old, Josie. I can't take those winters." Valerie shook her head.

"Please Mother. I hate to ask, I really do. I'll do all the driving and most of the work. I just need someone to help with the kids for a couple weeks while I get settled. Maybe do some of the cooking. Plus I need the moral support. Alice is too busy and she's helped us so much already," Josie pleaded.

"Well, if it's only two weeks, I guess I can do it. I don't even have any winter clothing," Valerie relented.

"Don't worry about that Mom. I'm going to order everything online for the kids, and I'll get you a hat, boots and gloves. I know your size. You can layer with the coat and sweaters you already have. It usually doesn't get much below the twenties anyway." Josie walked over to the play structure and helped Austen hang from the rings.

"What about the rest of your things? What about all the furniture?" Valerie called after her.

"I can't take anything else until the property settlement. All that stuff is community property. Richard is going to move back in as soon as I move out. I'm packing up all my personal stuff – my books and photos and stuff from before we were married, and storing it in the garage. I have an agreement with Richard that I can come and get it when I bring the kids back next summer."

"I'm selling my car to Kate, my next door neighbor," Josie continued. "She wants it for her nanny. We agreed on low blue book, which is all I'd get from a dealer. She's happy because she's driven with me and knows what a weenie driver I am. She also knows I'm an engineer and I believe in doing all the maintenance. She wants something safe and reliable because her kids will be in it." Josie grabbed Austen.

"Anyway, I have it all planned out. I'll buy a car when I get up to Montana. I'll have a few thousand from the old car and can get a loan from the credit union up there. I already checked it out. I'll need an all-wheel-drive, anyway. They only plow the main roads, remember? I don't want to be one of those people driving a California car in Montana and have everyone laugh at me when I get stuck in the snow."

Josie helped Austen onto the rings and let go as he hung by himself with two hands, proud and smiling. "Good grip," Valerie commented.

"He's so strong Mother. Phoebe couldn't hang by herself at this age." Josie lifted Austen from ring to ring before putting him down and gathering her things.

"Does Phoebe know she's moving in a few weeks?" Valerie asked as she walked to the car with her daughter and grandson.

"Not yet. I've been busy working out the details with Richard. He's so difficult. He does everything through the attorney. But the court accepted the report and I'm free to leave as soon as New Year's. I don't want to wait a minute longer."

"I know this has been hard on you, Josie, but I need to say it again: you're well rid of that man."

29

Phoebe put her arm around her little brother and they smiled adorably as Josie took their Christmas photo. It was just before Christmas, and Richard was due to pick them up for his last visit before the move.

"You guys are going to have Christmas Eve with Daddy, and then I'll pick you up and take you home. We'll have Christmas morning here like we always do. Just sit down until Daddy gets here." Josie put down her camera and picked up a letter she'd brought in from the mail box. *Another missive from Weiner,* she thought, tearing the envelope open.

"You are restrained from removing any community property from the Loranda residence upon your departure. You are allowed to take only personal property such as clothing….blah, blah, blah." Josie read the letter out loud before tossing it in the garbage. "Just the usual B.S.," she griped.

"Mom, you're not supposed to swear in front of us remember?" Phoebe said, reproaching her mother.

"Listen, Phoebe, sometimes you just have to close your ears. Also known as mind your own business. No comments from the peanut gallery etcetera. Anyway, all I said was B.S. – two little letters of the alphabet – it's hardly swearing."

"I know what B.S. means Mom, and it's swearing."

"Okay, Phoebe. Whatever. Just sit down next to your brother. Dad will be here soon enough." Josie wheeled their suitcase into the entry way.

It had been just over a year since Richard moved out and Josie was finally getting ready to move on with her life. After getting the house ready to sell earlier in the year, she'd closed up several of the rooms and put them off limits to the kids. She'd packed up her personal belongings and stacked them neatly in the garage. She was leaving the house spotless for Richard, not that he appreciated it. He would have all the appliances, linens, furniture and tools.

Before signing off her case, Josie's attorney had reminded her several times that she could only take personal items to Montana.

"Possession is nine-tenths of the law," Josie had protested. "I know what Richard is like. For all I know, he'll hide our stuff or give it away to his family. They have empty apartments in the city where he can stash stuff."

"You don't need to explain the law to me, Mrs. Bain. You aren't supposed to take anything that can be considered community property. He'll spend more money fighting you than the stuff is worth. It's all part of the game plan for guys like Richard. If you really want to make sure you get something, be sure to take pictures and document it. I'm sure Weiner will send a little reminder in any case."

Josie recalled the conversation she'd had with her attorney weeks earlier. True to form, Weiner had waited until two days before Christmas to send his little nasty gram. *Duly noted*, Josie thought to herself, *timing is everything when it comes to the war.* She made a note to herself to check out Weiner's social media pages to find out his birthday and favorite sports teams for when she needed to send him a nasty gram or two in the future.

The doorbell rang. "Dad's here," Phoebe announced listlessly. "Do I really have to go?" she pleaded.

"Yes, Phoebe, it's Christmas. You know how Grandma Bain is about Christmas. It's the single most important day of the year for her. She lives for Christmas. And you guys are the only grandchildren she has."

Josie thought about her mother-in-law's over-the-top devotion to Christmas and shook her head. No fewer than three Christmas trees lined her Hillsborough living room every year. Richard's mother could single handedly keep a half dozen Christmas stores in business. It wasn't about religion, unless you counted the religion of over-consumption.

"Sweetie, you'll have fun. You'll get nice presents," Josie cajoled her daughter.

"Last year Daddy only got presents for Austen!" Phoebe reminded Josie.

"Well, in any case you have to go. It's not optional. It's called a court order, and if I don't follow it I can get in big trouble." Josie held Phoebe's chin in her hand and caressed her hair as she looked her in the eyes.

Richard bounded into the house as soon as Josie cracked the door open. "Hey, wait on the porch. I'll bring the kids to you. This is still my home." Josie called after him as he pushed past her. "How are my kids?" Richard's voice boomed out as Phoebe and Austen shrank from his embrace.

Phoebe grabbed her brother's hand and dutifully led him out the door, pulling the suitcase behind her. Richard lingered on the porch and turned to Josie.

"This is temporary, Josie, so enjoy it while it lasts," he said. "I'll have custody by next Christmas and you can pick them up at my house for visitations. I'm getting remarried soon and the court always favors married couples over single mothers when it comes to child custody." He started to walk away.

"Thanks for the warning, Richard. I read the report. You'll need more than a new wife to convince the court to give you custody." Josie shook her head.

Richard turned to face her, his face red with rage. Josie went on the offensive. "You've been given so much, but you aren't grateful for anything. Instead of being happy you had a beautiful healthy daughter, you wasted no time telling me you wanted a son. When you finally got your son you were mean to him, too. Nothing that I or the kids ever did was good enough for you. I wasn't good enough, and the kids aren't good enough, either." Josie stopped to catch her breath.

"You're a narcissist! It's official! It's in the report!" She raised her voice. "The real problem isn't me and it isn't the kids – it's you!" Richard raised his arm as if to strike her. "Go ahead. I'll call the police." Josie held up her cell phone.

He put his arm down and walked away. Josie followed and saw Phoebe in the back seat watching her parents and crying. *I have to be more careful,* Josie thought, *he really brings out the worst in me.*

❦ 30 ❧

Josie saw the lights of her hometown in the distance as the plane descended into the valley. It was just past midnight on January second – the start of a new year and a new life. Austen was curled up on her lap, his seat belt loosely circling his body. Phoebe was across the aisle, her head on Valerie's shoulder.

"We're here, Mom," Josie whispered. "Wake up Phoebe and get her things together. Can you also take my purse? I'll have to carry Austen when we land." Josie straightened up and handed her purse to Valerie. She looked out her window at the snow flurries illuminated by the runway lights, as the attendants made their last trip through the cabin.

"How do you feel?" Valerie asked her, stretching her arms and yawning. "Are you happy to be back here?"

"I feel great. And yes, I'm happy to be back. I told Alice we'd get a taxi, but knowing her she'll probably be there waiting for us."

"You can watch the kids while I get the luggage. This is by far the most stuff I've ever checked. Everything we have to start our new life is stuffed into those bags." Josie carried Austen off the plane, while her mother and daughter followed.

Alice parked her car and went into the small regional airport. Standing behind a large group of people waiting to greet passengers, she quickly spotted Josie and waved. "How was the flight? Can I take anything?" Alice asked.

"Yes, you can take Austen," Josie said as she unloaded the sleeping toddler into Alice's arms. "I checked three massive bags. I hope there's room in the car for all of it."

"We'll squeeze in, no worries. I hope you guys brought some winter clothes." Alice immediately noticed that the kids were wearing tennis shoes and sweat shirts. "It's been in the teens, but it's supposed to go below zero tonight."

"Yep, I have everything," Josie said. "It's all planned out and organized. We had to change planes a couple times and I didn't want them to get too hot. I'll bring the bags over and get everything sorted out before we go out into the arctic blast."

"I'm getting cold just thinking about it." Valerie shivered.

Josie settled her family into the waiting area and went to get the luggage. She lifted a heavy bag off the conveyor belt and looked down to see Austen standing next to her. She carefully set it down. "Sweetie, you need to wait with grandma and sister. I know you want to help but these bags are too heavy for you." Alice ran over and grabbed the still-sleepy toddler.

Josie zipped open an over-sized bag and pulled out several new pair of winter boots as well as hats, gloves, mittens and down jackets stuffed into little sacks. She helped the kids into their new wardrobe, as Alice carried luggage to the car.

Phoebe and Austen, now fully awake, ran ahead as soon as their jackets were zipped. "Mom, it's snowing!" Phoebe shrieked. "I've never seen snow!" She held her mittens out and watched as snowflakes fell on them. Austen ran over to a snow bank twice his height and immediately tried to climb it.

"Come on kids, it's late. We've had a long day. We can play tomorrow. We're going to stay with Alice for a few days. She has a big yard and a sled and two really nice dogs. You guys will have a lot of fun." Josie stuffed the bags in the back and the family squeezed into the still-warm car.

"I can't begin to thank you for picking us up, Alice," Josie said, as she rubbed her hands together. "I've forgotten what cold air feels like. It really wakes you up. It's kind of refreshing actually." Alice started the car and headed towards the highway.

"Anyway, we'll only stay a few days. I still don't know if the apartment is ready. That property manager is used to dealing with Richard. God knows what Richard told him about me. But I'm the legal owner of the property so he has to listen to me now, and I don't like his attitude. He is really slow about returning my calls and claims he doesn't get my emails. He should be expecting me tomorrow, but we'll see."

Alice nodded as she drove into town.

"If the apartment isn't ready I'll move us into a hotel and get things sorted out. I know you don't have much room," Josie offered.

"It's fine, Josie. I set up beds in the basement. It's pretty cozy down there. Stay as long as you need to. You know you're always welcome," Alice reassured her friend.

Alice was the sister that Josie had never had. They'd helped each other through break-ups, and Josie had been there through Alice's own problems with an abusive husband and an ugly divorce.

❦ 31 ❧

"There are things I've never told anyone about Richard." Josie looked around at the familiar surroundings in her favorite hometown bakery, as Alice bit into a pastry. She'd gotten up early while her mother and the kids slept in after the late-night flight and had gone to have coffee with Alice before meeting with the property manager.

"Before we were married, two people warned me about him. The first one was a friend of a friend who'd worked with him on a job once, and the other one was a contractor I worked with, who had occasionally played on the same softball team as Richard. The contractor just shook his head when I told him I was marrying Richard. He said he hoped Richard wasn't still getting death threats."

Alice raised an eyebrow as Josie continued to talk. "So, it's not like there weren't a few red flags. But Richard always had a way of either explaining things away or just changing the subject."

"Josie, we all blow past red flags when we get into relationships. You never notice the stuff you don't want to see until it's too late and then you're kicking yourself." Alice shrugged.

"I have to go." Josie downed her coffee and stood. "I'm due at the apartment in five minutes. Wish me luck!"

Pulling up to her old apartment building, which a friend had once described as 'Victorian mansion meets Mid-western farmhouse,' Josie felt overjoyed. The place was even more beautiful than she remembered. Large and graceful, it had one of the best front porches in the neighborhood. She parked the rental car across the street and jogged over to meet her property manager, who was just getting out of his car.

"Hello, Mrs. Bain. The last tenants had to be evicted. We used the security deposit to clean the place up but there's still work to do." The manager was a tall, thin taciturn man who got right down to business.

"Why were they evicted?" This was the first Josie had heard about it. "College kids. There were a lot of complaints from the neighbors. They called the police numerous times, called the office. I told the kids to straighten up or they'd be evicted. The complaints kept coming, so we evicted. Being young males, they left the place a mess and after they got the notice they stopped paying the rent," he said matter-of-factly, walking up the steps.

"Did you ask the tenants what their side of the story was?" Josie asked.

"Yes, but you know how college kids are. They just blamed everything on the neighbors – a nice young couple – I know the family. There were numerous police reports documenting the problems. Anyway, it doesn't matter now." The manager opened the door and they stepped inside.

Josie looked around the front parlor. The exterior may have been Victorian, but the interior was authentic 1920s arts and crafts, with dark woodwork, large windows and expansive hardwood floors. "I see what you mean," Josie said, looking at the patched walls and grimy windows and floors.

"Obviously I have some work to do. I'll need help. Can you send one of your workers over for the rest of the week to help me patch, paint and clean? Also, how much was the cleaning deposit and what was is used for?" Now that Josie was finally dealing with this manager herself, she didn't like him. She had no way of knowing if the place had been touched since the students were evicted – it sure didn't look like it had been.

"Yes ma'am, we had a crew working over here all last week. I'll have to check the work orders and find out what they did. I know they re-keyed the doors and repaired a broken window. I think they also cleaned the appliances." She followed the manager into the kitchen. All Josie could see was grime. She opened the refrigerator and saw an old pizza box with stale pizza inside.

"Quite frankly it doesn't look as if anything was done," Josie said. "In any case, we need to move in by the end of the week so I can get the kids settled. Have your best worker over here at eight o'clock tomorrow morning. After we get settled, I'll stop by your office to review our contract." Josie was curt. The secretary had been nice enough to Josie the few times she'd called the office, but now that she was seeing firsthand how they had taken care of her property, she knew a change was in order.

"The good news is that the place is still beautiful. It's a spacious two bedroom apartment. I haven't been in there in years. I forgot how nice it was. It still has all the original woodwork and floors. It will clean up well." Josie was in Alice's kitchen helping Valerie cook dinner, while Alice was out walking her dogs.

"The bad news is that the last tenants were evicted and the place is a mess. The manager said they'd already blown through the security deposit but you wouldn't know it by looking. After we're settled I plan to tour all the properties and read through the management contract.

I may need to dump these guys. Maybe you can go with me, if you're still here, that is," Josie said.

"Josie, I know you're dealing with a lot – but do you have a plan for furniture?" Valerie asked.

"I don't know yet. Alice has a couple of twin beds in her garage she said she'd give me for the kids. I brought sleeping bags for everyone. The university is between semesters right now, and there's bound to be a lot of college kids ditching their stuff and leaving town. We can probably get some pretty good deals. A lot of east coast trust-funders come out to Montana for a semester with mom and dad's credit card, set up an apartment, buy a couch and a TV and then flunk out and leave. At least that's what used to happen when we lived here. A lot of times they don't even bother trying to sell the stuff – they just toss it in the alley or leave it in the apartment."

"I'd like to help you, Josie. I'd like to buy you some living room furniture to get you started in your new life," Valerie offered.

"Okay, Mom, but I still have all my stuff in Loranda. All that stuff is half mine. I just don't know how long the property settlement will take but I figured I can get by with a few things and by summer I'll finally get my stuff."

"You need to face facts, Josie." Valerie stopped what she was doing to face her daughter. "Richard isn't going to let you get any of that stuff. Mark my words. He'll get the house and everything in it. There won't be a moving van coming to Montana with your things. I bit my tongue when you told me what the lawyer said about leaving everything. She gave you bad advice. The only chance you had to get any of your things was when you were still in the house. Like it or not, you're starting over from scratch now."

"You saw the letter from Weiner. He threatened me. I had to leave everything." Josie was defensive but she had a sick feeling that her mother was right. Valerie shrugged and went to set the table.

❦ 32 ❦

Smoke from the self-cleaning oven lingered in the air as Josie scrubbed out the refrigerator. A worker from the management company was in the living room changing light bulbs in the hundred-year-old chandelier.

There was a knock at the door. "Hello - anyone home?" A woman in ski pants and dark glasses called out as she stepped into the house.

"Just a minute," Josie answered from the kitchen. The visitor was just taking off her boots when Josie came out to greet her.

"Hi, I'm Francine!" The woman smiled brightly and held out her hand to Josie. "I live upstairs with my husband, Beau. Are you the new tenant?" she asked.

"Yes, we're just moving in. I'm Josie. I'll be here with my two kids. I'm also the owner of the building. Nice to meet you." Josie shook the woman's hand.

"Where are you moving from?" Francine asked.

"We're from the Bay Area. A suburban town called Loranda," Josie replied.

"That's amazing!" Francine exclaimed. "I used to teach in Loranda. I was the substitute art teacher at the high school when the regular teacher went on maternity leave a few years ago. Small world!" Francine smiled at Josie and looked around the room.

"Well then we'll have a lot to talk about. Wait until I tell the kids. My kids are still young – Phoebe is my third grader and Austen is almost four."

"Do you mind if I look around? We've been living upstairs for three years but I've never been in this apartment. It's gorgeous." Francine ran her hand over the carved wood in the entry way. "We're so glad to have a family moving in. It's just been one group of college kids after another since we moved here. The last group got evicted. They were pretty nice guys, though. I assume they didn't pay the rent or something."

"So I heard," Josie said. "Well, never fear, we're here now and things should start to settle down."

Francine walked through the apartment. "It's huge – look at all this room!" She exclaimed.

"Yes it's definitely spacious – but right now there are only two bedrooms. My kids are still young so I can put them in the same room for now, but eventually I'll have to figure something out. I'd offer you a cup of coffee but..." Josie motioned to the empty apartment.

"Actually, I'm ready for a break – do you want to get some coffee?" Josie was ready to head back to her favorite bakery after working at the apartment all morning. Growing up, Penelope's bakery was the place she hung out with her friends, and she still considered it ground zero in her hometown.

"Thanks for the invite but I'm on my way to meet my husband. We're headed up to the ski hill – twelve inches of new powder up there today. But, it was great meeting you. Wow, I can't believe you lived in Loranda! Let's have coffee tomorrow. When you're ready for a break just ring my bell." Francine put her boots back on and left.

"Mommy, when will Luke get here?" Austen was very attached to the family's three year old Border collie. Josie was back at Alice's house after spending the day cleaning the family's new apartment and she realized the time had come to tell Austen and Phoebe about Luke. Richard had informed her that he had no intention of taking care of the family dog even temporarily, despite the fact that they'd adopted him together. Amidst the legal and financial struggles of the previous year, Josie had made the agonizing decision to return Luke to the rescue group they'd adopted him from. Her future was uncertain and she knew they couldn't keep Luke in an apartment that lacked a fenced yard. A few days before they left for Montana she'd driven Luke back to the ranch where she'd adopted him and gave the rescue group the biggest donation she could afford. The day after they arrived in Montana she'd received an email from the rescue group saying that Luke had been adopted by a new family.

"Sweetheart, Luke will be staying in California. He can't live here with us because he needs a big yard with a fence and we don't have one anymore. And he probably wouldn't like all this snow anyway." Josie picked up Austen and put him on her hip. "I want Luke to come here, Mommy. I miss Luke." The little boy started to cry.

"Austen, don't cry," Phoebe said, reaching up to touch Austen. "Luke will live with Daddy at our old house and he will be there when we visit. Right, Mommy?" Phoebe asked.

"Um, okay, I guess we need to talk about this now. So, I had to take Luke back to the ranch where we got him. Remember the nice lady where we got him, Phoebe? Well, I took him back there and they found a new home for him." Phoebe's eyes filled with tears.

"Why did you do that, Mommy? Why couldn't he stay with Daddy so we could still see him?" Phoebe ran out of the room while Austen continued to sob in Josie's arms.

"I'm sorry kids. It was a hard decision. But I had to do what was best for Luke. He needs a home with a big yard and we don't have that anymore. After we're settled we can all go together and look at puppies. We need a small dog that can live in an apartment and go on walks. We also need a Montana dog – one that's used to the snow." She hugged Austen again. "I'm sorry."

"Yay! We're get to have a puppy!" Austen suddenly jumped out of her arms and ran off to tell his sister.

"I didn't say for sure we'd get a puppy – I only said we'd look." Josie called after him.

Valerie put down her paper and started to laugh. "You know you can't tell a four-year-old that you're only going to 'look' at puppies. You've as good as promised him a puppy, Josie. Now you're going to be dealing with puppy piddle along with everything else." Valerie shook her head.

The outside gate banged shut and Alice came in through the back door, stomping snow off her boots. "Has there been any word on your dog, Josie? Is Richard going to ship him up to Montana after you get settled?"

"Funny you should ask." Josie and Valerie looked at each other. "We were just talking about that. I didn't want to tell you earlier, Alice, but I decided to take him back the rescue group. And even though I'm basically broke, I gave them a nice donation while I was there. He's still young and we trained him pretty well. I just got an email from them – turns out he was adopted immediately by another family."

"Wow, Josie – I told you he could have stayed here with me as long as you needed."

"I know – and I'm grateful for all your help, Alice – but honestly, it was just one more thing I couldn't deal with. Richard flat out refused to take care of him, even temporarily. I also knew we couldn't keep him up here since we wouldn't have a fenced yard."

"Well, I still wish you'd just brought him with you. I have room for another dog," Alice said, sitting down to untie her boots.

"I know, but we also had a ton of luggage and with my mom and the kids and the snow, I just didn't think I could manage the dog also." Josie shrugged.

Austen and Phoebe ran into the room, both yelling at the same time. "Mom's gonna get us a puppy! Mom's gonna get us a puppy!"

Alice looked at her friend. "Is that true?"

"Austen – you know I said we'd go and look at puppies. We might get one but I didn't say for sure. I just said we'd look. Famous last words, I know," Josie said as the kids ignored her.

"I want a boxer!" Phoebe cried. "I want a boy dog! I want a big dog!" Austen yelled.

"Well, you really stepped in it now, Josie. Looks like you're going to end up with a puppy to deal with." Alice smiled and walked into the kitchen.

"That's what I told her," Valerie piped up. "Well, if you do decide to get a puppy let me help you. A friend of mine has a rez dog rescue operation up at Flathead. She goes to the reservation and rescues stray dogs. I know she gets puppies, too. Would you guys like a rez dog puppy? They're fluffy and cute," Alice asked Austen and Phoebe.

"Yes! Alice please talk mom into a puppy!" Phoebe pleaded.

"Most of the dogs on the reservation are lucky to live a year. I adopted Kirby, my shepherd mix, from the rez last year. He was a real fixer-upper but he's a great dog – aren't you Kirby? Aren't you,

you rascal? When I got him he had mange and part of his tail was missing from frostbite." Alice nuzzled her dog.

"Wow, Alice. Frost bite? Mange? Really? We're used to those pampered California suburban dogs. You go to the dog park down there and it's usually all purebreds."

Josie tucked the kids into their beds and headed back up to the living room where her mother and her best friend were sitting in front of the fireplace, chatting over cups of tea.

"I need help with this dream I had recently. I keep thinking about it," Josie said as she sat down on the couch.

"I was up in the mountains following this enormous brown bear and he was talking to me. I looked down below me and it was a sheer cliff. There was a canyon with a river, and Richard and Weiner and some other people were there. I think they were people from Richard's family or from Weiner's office or something. I looked at them and they all had guns. They didn't see me up on the trail."

Josie got up and poured herself a cup of tea. "The bear was like 'you need to take the high road,' and then I looked down and there was a bow and arrow lying there. I was sitting on a rock looking out into the canyon, and the bear was standing nearby. I took the bow and arrow and shot one arrow down at Weiner and Richard. Just as soon as I let go of my one arrow there were suddenly a million arrows flying through the sky. Then the bear told me the only weapon I had was my words. I don't remember what happened next but it was something about using my words. My words are my weapons."

"Well, you're back in Griz country," Alice said, referring to the local football team. "So I think the bear is pretty obviously a reference to Montana. And let's face it, you're outgunned. Richard has a lot of money and you're basically out of money."

"That reminds me." Josie sat up. "My attorney sent me a form to sign saying that I'm taking over my own case. I haven't signed it. I haven't written her back. Honestly, I just couldn't deal with it, getting ready for the move and everything. Plus, I still owe her money."

"You have to deal with it, Josie. This is exactly what Richard's plan was all along. It's a standard war tactic – starve them out. He figured you'd run out of money and you'd have to go to court alone. Then he'd offer you his chump change settlement and you'd have no option but to take it. I'll help you with this. Tim said he'd be happy to give you free legal advice as long as he stays in the background," Alice said.

"The only reason I still feel okay about helping you pay that attorney is that it got you out of your marriage," Valerie added. "But that money sure disappeared fast. Anyway, I'm now convinced that this is a good move for you and the kids. Don't get me wrong – I'd love to have you closer to me – but the schools here are excellent and there's a lot of things for the kids to do. They'll be spending more time outdoors sledding, skiing and building snowmen. In California they'd be watching TV while it rained all winter. And you'll be able to get back on your feet living in your own apartment building." Valerie put an arm around her daughter and gave her a hug.

"Alice is right," Valerie continued. "You're going to have to take over the case yourself. I'll help with furniture and incidentals. You're an educated woman, Josie – you're every bit as smart as those smarmy attorneys."

"I'm starting to know why people hate lawyers. And the rest of the divorce industry – don't get me started…" Josie said.

"I don't think you should include Dr. Stokes, Josie. He gave you a move-away. You know the court never would have done that." Valerie reminded her daughter.

"I feel like I worked for that move-away, Mom. I worked my butt off. But I admit I also got lucky when Richard showed the guy what an ass he really is. I paid for it too, because now I don't get to have my kids on Christmas or Thanksgiving. Anyway, what do you guys think about my dream?"

"Well, it's interesting to me that you think the bear symbolizes Montana." Valerie said turning to Alice. "I immediately thought it symbolized California. Isn't the bear the state symbol – it's on the flag."

"There used to be thousands of brown bears – grizzly bears really – in California," Valerie continued. "Probably at least as many as were here in Montana. Maybe the bear is a dual symbol – reflecting Josie's roots in both states."

"I went through divorce in Montana and it was nothing like what Josie's going through. The whole process is fairer. The divorce industry hasn't taken over yet – probably because most people up here don't have the money to shovel at it. I grew up in San Diego and I'm a native Californian, but I never would have believed how corrupt and money-driven the courts have become if I hadn't been going through it with Josie." Alice shook her head.

"So they have the guns and all I have are words. Great." Josie continued. "What's the deal with the bow and arrow? Oh – now I remember – the bear was leaving me and he said to make every word an arrow and to let arrows fill the sky."

"It's a beautiful image, Josie. A million arrows raining down on Richard and Weiner – truly a dream come true," Alice laughed.

"The bear also said to take the high road. So I have to take the high road and somehow defend myself against the big guns using only my words."

"You know what they say, Josie – the pen is mightier than the sword. You have to start writing. As soon as you get settled you need to set up a place to work and start writing. Paper the court with your words. Turn your words into arrows and aim every one of them at Richard and Weiner and the court. Fill up sky with arrows."

Alice went to get a pen and paper, while Valerie left to go to bed.

"Actually, there's no time like the present. We can start getting organized now." Alice sat down with her note pad, suddenly feeling energized. "Don't forget, Josie - this is war. We have to plan, strategize and out-maneuver the enemy. Richard already thinks you're toast. He figures there's no way you'll be up to the task."

"He's right, Alice. I am toast. I'm not up to this. I can't do it. Give me a differential equation to solve. Tell me to project manage a pump station installation. Don't tell me to figure out how to file motions and argue my case in court. Ain't going to happen. I don't have it in me."

"You of all people can't afford to go negative." Alice said. "If you continue to think those negative thoughts you really are toast. You may as well sign everything you own over to Richard right now. Oh, and you may as well drop the kids off with him too – because you're going to fight that battle again, guaranteed."

"Well, at least let me finish getting moved in to the house." Josie pleaded as she headed downstairs to go to bed.

∽ 33 ∾

Josie waited patiently as the new puppy sniffed the bike rack in front of the building next door. The apartment house next door was a bright yellow blight on the neighborhood, and she'd always vowed to buy it someday, if only to paint it a decent color.

Parked in front of the bright yellow building, was a bright yellow car. As she walked past the building she saw a man in a bright yellow rain jacket walking towards her.

"Hey - are you the new neighbor?" The man walked up to Josie. He was about her height with thick curly dark blond hair and an easy, gregarious manner.

"Yes, I'm Josie," she answered, holding out a mittened hand for him to shake.

"Good to meet you, Josie. I'm Iggy," he said, shaking her hand.

"Don't tell me you live in this building and drive that yellow car," Josie said, half-joking.

"Yep. That's me. I didn't plan it that way. I've had that car for years and I've had this jacket almost as long." Iggy shrugged.

"Well, points for consistency I guess," Josie said.

"So – is this your dog?" Iggy bent down to pet the black and white puppy. "I heard it whining the other day. You know it's a cow dog don't you? It'll be totally insane for the first three years but then it'll settle down."

"Uh, thanks for the warning. Actually she's from the reservation. The kids picked her out."

"You have kids? How old are they?" Iggy asked, standing back up. "I'm Paul's dad. He's that curly-haired three-year-old you've probably seen running around here. Is that little blond guy yours? Paulie rang your bell the other day, looking for that kid." Iggy smiled at his tall slender neighbor with the expensive boots and long cashmere coat.

Josie recalled her surprise a few days earlier, when a small boy with a mass of curly dark hair spilling out of his snow cap stood alone on her front porch incessantly ringing her door bell. Only three years old, he was almost a year younger than her son and small for his age.

Oh great, a feral child in the neighborhood, she'd thought. As soon as she opened the door the boy slipped past her and ran straight into the Phoebe and Austen's bedroom, as if he lived there. Austen was surprised and amused when the bold younger boy burst into his room and ran up to him, without the slightest trace of inhibition. Austen looked at the boy then looked at Josie before shrugging his shoulders and introducing himself at Josie's prompting.

"Is your son the little guy with the dark curly hair?" She asked Iggy.

"Yep, that's him."

"It's just that I'm not used to having three-year-olds ring my door bell without a parent or nanny around. I'm used to having parents arrange play-dates, and of course at this age there's always an adult around."

"Play-dates? Really? That's the biggest load of crap I've ever heard. We just call it going out to play." Iggy shook his head.

"I'm not saying I agree with it. Actually, I think a lot of the parents where we used to live were pretty stuck up. I felt like I needed to provide a full dossier on my child before they'd let their kid play with mine. I'm actually from here, but I left when I was seventeen." Josie liked this guy. He was off-hand and funny. She also thought he was sexy.

"So what do you do? Are you from here?" Josie continued walking her puppy around the block as her neighbor fell in step beside her.

"I have a ranch in the Bitterroot but my wife talked me into moving into town last year so she could go back to college and get her degree. Turned out she was having an affair with her professor and she filed for divorce. She threw me out of the house."

A short time after Paul came over to play that day, a petite, dark-haired woman in a very short skirt also rang Josie's bell. She'd introduced herself as Paul's mother, Beth. She looked about nineteen, but she could have been older, it was hard to tell.

"So is Beth your wife? She came over a few days ago."

"That's her. The bitch. She threw me out so she could be with her professor, but then I heard that he ditched her. Serves her right," Iggy said, agitated.

"It sounds sort of toxic. Don't get me wrong – I'm not judging you – my situation isn't any better – worse actually." Josie looked closely at Iggy's face and judged him to be in his forties. "But, isn't she a little young for you? I mean she looked like she was barely twenty."

"She's twenty-eight. Twenty years younger than me. We've been together ten years, married for three." Iggy stuffed his hands in his pockets as he walked.

"Yeah, she looked really young, but when I talked to her she seemed a lot older. In fact, my first impression is that you guys are opposites. You have a young vibe and she has an old vibe. It's like she's an old person stuck in a young body and you're a young person stuck in an – uh – older body."

"That's good, Josie. I like that. That sums it up pretty well. Anyway, we're divorced now. She's not my wife anymore. The divorce was final last month. Last summer my life was perfect, beautiful wife, awesome kid, and six months later it's over. Things can change overnight." Iggy's voice started to break.

They'd rounded the block and were back in front of the yellow building. Noticing that he was getting emotional, Josie gently placed a hand on his shoulder.

"Listen, Iggy. I'm going through the big D myself. I know what it's like. If you ever need to talk I'm right next door." Josie picked up the puppy and walked back to her own house. As she opened the door she glanced over at her new neighbor. Iggy smiled and slowly waved as she went inside and closed the door.

That evening, Josie made an extra pizza and called the kids into the kitchen. "Phoebe, you and Austen can take this next door to the yellow apartments. Take it to apartment number three. Tell him it's from us, next door. Tell him I need the plate back when he's done." Josie handed Phoebe a plate covered with foil.

"Can we make a snowman after that?" Phoebe asked.

"Of course. Just stay in the yard so I can see you." Phoebe took the plate and ran out the door, her brother close behind.

One of Josie's family rituals was making pizza on Friday afternoon. Her usual recipe called for letting the dough rise in a warm spot, which had been easy when she lived in California. Every window in the house had sunlight streaming through it at some point during the day. Her Montana home wasn't lacking in windows, in fact there were large elegant windows throughout the apartment, but very little sunlight streamed through them, especially in the winter.

She'd improvised and baked the pies without letting the dough rise. To her surprise she couldn't tell the difference, the pizzas were just as good. She decided to make one extra in case Alice stopped by, but gave it to her heartbroken, good-looking neighbor instead.

Josie stretched out on the couch and watched the kids play in front of her house. It was barely a week since they'd moved in and the neighborhood gang had already formed. In addition to Austen, Phoebe and Paul, there was five-year-old Maggie, whose nanny was Francine the upstairs neighbor, and Joseph, another inhabitant of the yellow apartment building next door, who was the same age as Phoebe.

Francine was an artist who also worked part time as a nanny for a wealthy ranch family and often brought Maggie to her apartment after school. Maggie and Phoebe rolled a giant snowball to make the base of the snowman, while Paul and Austen chased Joseph around the yard.

The boys pelted Iggy with snowballs as he walked past, carrying the empty pizza dish. Josie saw him coming and opened the door just as the bell rang.

"Will you marry me?" Iggy smiled and walked into the house without being asked. He handed the plate to Josie.

"I guess that means you liked the pizza. Thanks for bringing the plate back. I still don't have my stuff from California. We have just enough plates to get through the day around here." Josie followed Iggy into the dining room.

"This place is nice. Very posh. I could see myself in a place like this." Iggy looked around. "It reminds me of a place where I stayed in London once."

"Thanks. We like it. It's really different from what we're used to. It's big enough but I don't have separate rooms for the kids." Josie said. Iggy walked to the back of the house and looked at the bedrooms.

He went into the kitchen and stepped into the over-sized pantry next to the breakfast nook.

"I lived on a sailboat for ten years. That's actually how I met Beth but that's another story. Anyway, what I learned from living on a yacht was you don't really need a lot of room." He looked around the pantry and paced it off. "This space is plenty big enough for Austen. He'd probably be happy in here. And you aren't using it anyway, from the looks of it." The room was empty except for some shelves on the wall.

"Just think 'boat cabin,'" Iggy told her. "You can get a standard twin sized bed in here but you'll have to get a carpenter to build it custom. I have just the guy for you. I'll get you his card. You can put the bed here, and get him to build you some shelves and drawers over there." Iggy pointed and motioned as he described the new bedroom. "It'll be great." He flashed Josie a smile.

"Wow, Iggy. I like it. I really wasn't sure what I was going to do in here. The manager said it was a pantry, but it's way too big for a pantry. I'll call your friend and see what he says. I'm on a budget, but it beats having to move again." Josie smiled.

Standing close to Iggy in this small room, Josie noticed his smooth, strong hands. He noticed her looking at him. Never one to miss an opportunity, he took a step closer. "You have beautiful hair," he told her, looking into her eyes.

"Thanks," she said as she backed out of the room. "Well, I'm glad you liked the pizza. I can make us lattes – would you like one?" Josie offered.

"I'll take a beer." Iggy followed her into the kitchen.

"Okay, a beer. I hope you don't mind if it isn't cold." She searched for two glasses. Iggy put his arm around her waist and pulled her to him.

"You're attractive, don't get me wrong," Josie said, breaking free. "But this is just too soon for me Iggy. Really. I don't want to get involved right now. It's just..." Iggy put his arms around her again.

"You want to, Josie, don't deny it." He moved a strand of hair from her face and started to kiss her.

Josie stepped out of his arms. "It's not that. I'm just not comfortable. And to be honest, I noticed how upset you were when I asked you about your wife earlier. I think you're still hung up on her. I don't want to be your rebound girlfriend. We live too close for that. Also you're kind of G.U. – geographically unsuitable. And besides, we've barely met." She handed Iggy a beer and a glass and walked into the dining room.

"That's funny; I thought being next door neighbors made us very geographically suitable, Josie. You're not giving me a chance." Iggy walked behind her as he poured himself a beer.

"We'll see. Anyway, here's to the guy with the bright yellow car, the bright yellow house and bright yellow personality. Cheers." Josie lifted her glass to Iggy.

❦ 34 ❦

Phoebe waved to her mother as the school bus pulled away from the curb, her warm breath fogging up the small window. Josie walked slowly back to her house. The sky was gray and the snow was crusted over and icy. She entered the darkened house, not bothering to open the drapes as she usually did. She walked past the pile of manila envelopes and express mailers that spilled across the dining room table, unopened.

It had been several weeks since they'd moved in and their lives had settled into routine. Phoebe was in school, Austen was in part-time pre-school and Josie was in divorce litigation hell. The novelty of building snowmen and meeting new neighbors had worn off, and the soul-crushing reality of her situation with Richard and Weiner bore down on her.

She peeked into the converted pantry she'd turned into a perfect little boy-cave, and saw Austen wrapped up in his blankets; sound asleep with the black and white puppy curled up at his feet. Josie went into her bathroom and turned on the shower. She looked in the mirror briefly before slumping against the wall and sliding down to the floor.

Her cell phone went off. It was a text from Alice: "WHERE ARE YOU? CALL ME." She powered the phone down and tossed it back into the bedroom. Crying always gave Josie a headache, and even when things were difficult the tears usually refused to come. She hadn't shed one tear since her whole ordeal had begun. When she first met Iggy, he told that he cried for months after his marriage ended. He told her there was something wrong with her because she hadn't cried once throughout her divorce.

She was crying now. Her knees pulled up to her body, and her face in her hands, she cried. Slowly she slipped off her shoes and began to undress. She crawled into the shower and sat under the steaming hot water, lifting her face to wash away the tears. She stayed there until the water ran cold.

"Mommy? Where are you, Mommy?" Austen appeared in the bathroom.

"Mommy's in the shower, sweetie. Just wait a few minutes. I'll get you breakfast when I get out. You can watch TV." Austen ran into the living room and turned on the TV, with the puppy at his heels.

Josie wrapped a towel around her and looked in the mirror. Her eyes were red and swollen, with heavy dark bags underneath them. There were lines on her face she'd never noticed before. Her hair was streaked with gray and she couldn't remember the last time she'd washed and conditioned it. She'd lost weight, but not in a good way. She hadn't worked out in months and had lost all the muscle tone on her arms and legs that she used to be so proud of.

I'm a mess. She thought. *I need to pull myself together.* She started to cry again. Bending over, she tried to comb through her wet matted hair, before giving up and tying it into a messy bun. She wrapped her bathrobe around her still-wet body and put her feet into her slippers before going into the kitchen to make oatmeal for her son.

"Is your mom here?" She heard Iggy's bright voice in the living room. She'd forgotten how informal things were in Montana. She felt like she was living in a sitcom where characters just let themselves into her house unannounced. One minute she was alone in the kitchen making oatmeal, wearing nothing but a bathrobe, and the next minute her neighbor was standing next to her, pouring a cup of coffee and chatting about the weather.

"Oh, Iggy. It's you. Hi." Josie said listlessly, the sound of cartoons playing in the background. Iggy walked into the kitchen.

"Austen, could you please turn that down? Mommy has a headache." She filled a small bowl with oatmeal and covered it with brown sugar. She poked at it and stirred it a little before taking it out to the living room. Iggy followed her.

"You're depressed, babe. Really, you need to get out of this house. It's depressing. I'm taking Paul skiing this afternoon – do you and Austen want to come? The boys would love it."

"I haven't skied in years, Iggy. I forgot how. Besides, I don't have any gear." Josie shrugged. She didn't even have the energy to get dressed let alone go skiing.

"What's all this stuff?" Iggy picked up one of the express mail packages and looked at the label. "Diablo Valley Law Firm," he read out loud.

"Thanks, Iggy. I can read." Josie sat Austen up straight on the couch and put a tea towel on his lap before handing him his oatmeal, his eyes never leaving the TV screen.

"Shouldn't you be opening this stuff? What's going on with the lawyer anyway? Are you working on the settlement?" Iggy peppered her with questions.

"What lawyer? There is no lawyer, Iggy. It's just me. The lawyer sent me some form to sign and now the only time I hear from her is when she sends me her bill every month. It keeps getting bigger because I can't afford to pay it."

"That sucks. What's your plan? Do you want me to help you go through all this stuff?" He pulled out a chair and sat down. "My divorce was simple compared to yours. The only thing we owned together was the car and some furniture. I gave her the car and told her to take whatever furniture she wanted. I wanted her to have a decent car since she's driving my kid around. The ranch was mine long before we met; it's been in the family for years." Iggy paused and picked up another letter.

"I've dealt with lawyers before. I can at least help you sort through this stuff." Iggy pulled the tab on one of the mailers.

It'd been weeks since Josie signed the substitution of attorney that allowed her lawyer to get off her case. Nearly every day since then an express mail truck had pulled up in front of her house. Each time, a middle-aged woman in a black uniform got out of the truck and rang Josie's doorbell. Every time the woman rang the doorbell, Josie came to answer it. Day after day, the woman had another package for Josie. Each day Josie signed her name then the woman handed her the package, thanked her and left. Josie tossed each package onto the growing pile on her dining room table.

Then one day the woman spoke to Josie. "What are all these packages anyway? Are they checks?" Josie looked at the woman for a long moment before she burst out laughing. She laughed and laughed. She was bent over laughing.

"Checks? You think these are checks? Hahahaha…" Josie laughed some more.

"What's so funny?" The woman said.

"Well, I'm sorry to disappoint you. These aren't checks." Josie caught her breath. "Noooo, these are love letters from my ex-husband's attorney."

"Oh honey, I'm so sorry." The woman reached out to touch Josie's hand.

"Oh, it's okay. If they stopped coming I'd wonder if he still loved me," Josie said wryly.

She figured Weiner really should love her, since he was already into Richard for at least fifty thousand dollars. Where would Weiner be without the Josie's of the world to beat up on? She often pictured the first meeting between Richard and Weiner. "I want to destroy my wife." She imagined Richard saying.

"'Well sir, you've come to the right place." Weiner would rub his hands together and answer with a smug, smarmy smile on his face. "Cost is no issue." Richard would say. "This is war." Richard would be serious and solemn.

"That's just what I like to hear." Weiner would respond, walking around his dark, polished mile-long desk to shake Richard's hand. "This is war and you've just found your general. We've never lost a war yet, Mr. Bain." Then the men would shake hands and laugh.

Weiner's website featured pictures of loving mothers and fathers playing with their smiling children, and prominently advertised his claim that he's a 'family law specialist who puts the interests of his client's families first.' Somehow Josie missed the part where it mentioned the word 'war.'

Goody goody, Richard would think as he drove home from his first meeting with Weiner. His fantasy was about to come true. Too cowardly to enlist in the military and possibly have to fight a real war, Richard was the type of guy who relished the thought of a war that he knew he could win – a war against an unemployed, forty-year-old woman with no family money behind her. A war against the mother of his children. His very own weenie war.

Josie sat down next to Iggy and picked up one of the packages. "I wonder what this cost? It's at least twenty bucks to send it express mail, and probably a few hundred dollars a page. I saw Weiner's fees – five hundred bucks an hour," she said.

"Anyway, yes it would be good if you helped me Iggy. I know I have to open them. Just give me a little time. I need to get dressed." She got up and left the room. Josie closed her bedroom door, took off her robe and put on some leggings. She pulled a sweater over her head and splashed some water on her face before she walked back into the dining room. Iggy had poured her a cup of coffee.

"You've been crying," Iggy observed.

"I know. I'm not crying because I miss Richard or because I'm sad about the divorce or anything like that. I'm crying because I can't deal with having to go to court alone. I spent all the money my mom gave me and I maxed out two credit cards paying the stupid attorney and I'm no closer to a settlement than I ever was."

"No point in feeling sorry for yourself, babe. It sucks, but moping around here letting the whole thing pile up doesn't help anything. You have to take back your power. You gave your power away to the attorney and now you need to take it back." Iggy took both her hands in his and squeezed them for emphasis.

"I don't have anyone, Iggy. He has an entire law firm and his money-bags mother behind him. I have nothing," Josie said with self-pity in her voice.

"I'm not nothing. Alice isn't nothing. Tim isn't nothing. Your mom isn't nothing. He has Weiner and you have your mom and your friends. We're not nothing and we'll help you get through this." Iggy scolded her as he sorted the envelopes into piles.

Josie brightened up. "You're right, Iggy. I gave away my power and I have to take it back. You guys are my legal team now. An unemployed engineer, an elderly woman, a graphic designer, a middle school math teacher and her boyfriend who works as an attorney for the reservation." She pulled a legal brief out of one of the envelopes and sipped her coffee. "That should work."

"I had this dream the other day. I was out in a canyon somewhere and there was a sheer granite wall that went up as far as I could see. Richard was standing with his back against the wall. There was a roaring fire all around him. A giant inferno. He was completely surrounded on all sides with a granite wall at his back. Flames were flickering all around him and starting to lick at his face. Embers were blowing into his hair. He stood there motionless. Suddenly, the flames parted and a giant hand reached through them. The hand gave Richard a pen and paper and told him to sign the document." Iggy stopped what he was doing and waited to hear the rest of the dream.

"Then the dream ended. I don't know what happened next. I don't know if Richard signed the paper or not," Josie said anti-climactically.

"Wow, Josie. That's not a dream. That's a scene from a B movie or something. You aren't a Scorpio by any chance are you?" Iggy looked at her over his glasses.

"You know I'm not into new-age B.S. and I don't watch B movies. In fact, I don't have time to watch any movies." Josie concentrated on the papers in front of her. "It's funny though, I took you for a new-age hippie when I first met you. Good guess about the Scorpio thing. You probably saw my birth date somewhere."

"Actually, I think you're too nice to be a Scorpio, but Beth pegged you for one. She's very intuitive about those things." Iggy shrugged. "Anyway, whatever you are, you need to take back your power and never ever give it to anyone else ever again. And don't hold your breath about Richard signing any agreement. I think the dream is trying to tell you something: even with his back against a granite wall and surrounded by flames he isn't going to settle. He will only do it when he's ordered by a judge. The only thing Richard will sign is complete capitulation on your part. You give him everything. All the property, the kids, everything."

"That's what I'm afraid of, Iggy. My attorney told me to forget trying to settle. This is going to trial. And I couldn't afford to pay what I owed, much less pay for her to take it to trial. So I'm going to trial against Richard and Weiner. You're right about taking back my power. That's the best thing you could have said to me. You're better than any of the therapists I've been to. I feel better already." Josie smiled brightly at her friend and sipped some coffee.

∞ 35 ∞

Snow flurries swirled around the sidewalk outside the window of the neighborhood bakery, while Josie sat at a corner table holding her coffee cup with both hands. The warm cup sent a shiver down her spine. The door banged open, and Alice walked in wearing a heavy sweater and jeans.

"Stay there," she said to Josie. "I'll just grab something and be right back." She set her hat and gloves down on the chair next to Josie and went to the counter to order a sandwich.

"How long have you been here?" She asked as she sat down with her sandwich.

"Not long. I'm taking a break. Austen's at his new pre-school for a couple hours. I finally started looking through all those legal filings Weiner's bombarded me with. There are eighteen separate mailers full of legal stuff. Bastard. I glanced at one of them and it was full of statements like 'Respondent deliberately deprives Petitioner of the children. Respondent has been diagnosed with mental illness. Blah, Blah, Blah...' I feel like I need someone to hold my hand while I go through this stuff. It's just lies and garbage. Maybe if you pre-read them for me and let me know what they said first – to sort of screen them for me. Sorry to be such a wuss, Alice."

"No problem. That's what friends are for. I'll stop by this evening and we can sit down and go through them. I'm just glad to see you're up and about. I was worried about you. I stopped by the house several times and no one answered. I went around the side and looked in the windows – all the drapes were pulled shut. Did you get my texts?" Alice took a bite of her sandwich as she eyed her friend closely.

"Yes, I got the texts. I was in bad shape. Just really depressed. I didn't even get dressed for days. I put on my bathrobe and walked Phoebe to the bus in the morning. I put my coat on over my PJs and went shopping, hoping I didn't bump into anyone. If it wasn't for Iggy I'd still be in my gloomy house wallowing and crying. He said something that got me to snap out of it. I don't know how he did it but it worked."

"Well, that's good. Who is this guy anyway? Iggy? Are you seeing him?" Alice slid her plate towards Josie and motioned for her to take the other half of the sandwich while she took another bite herself.

"He's a neighbor. About my height. Curly blond hair. His ex is tiny, looks like she's thirteen." Josie paused. "Part of me is interested, but the other part says 'don't go there, Josie.' For one thing he's right next door, and for another he's still hung up on his ex. He denies it, but from the way he talks about her I know he's not over her. He's probably one of those guys who get over heartbreak by getting laid or by finding some rebound relationship." Josie reached over and picked up the other half sandwich.

"Plus, I don't know how to manage a relationship being a single mom. The other day he came over and sat on the couch next to me. Close, but not touching. Maybe our arms were touching, slightly. His son Paul was playing on the floor with Austen and we were just sitting there, halfheartedly watching a movie. Suddenly Phoebe walks into the room and deliberately stomps over and squeezes her little butt right in between us, forcing us apart. Then she crosses her arms and just turns and gives Iggy this look – sort of like 'stay away from my mom.' It was pretty rude actually. I was shocked at her behavior," Josie said.

Alice laughed. "I always knew Phoebe was a smart kid. It seems like she has good taste in men, too. Or at least she's figured out that her mom has terrible taste in men." Alice laughed again. "I think I remember him. I came over looking for you one day and he was outside loading his skis into his car – over by the yellow apartments. Started to chat me up right away. Not bad looking but, let's face it, Josie, he's obviously a player."

"Hey – that's not exactly fair. Except for Richard I have pretty good taste in men," Josie objected.

Alice laughed some more. "Okay, whatever you say."

"What do you know about him anyway? What is he forty-five? Fifty? He probably has a lot of baggage. I still remember your good-looking college boyfriend – Iggy's the same type of guy - a total player." Alice shook her head.

"Whatever. We're just friends. His kid is a year younger than Austen and they've become besties. Iggy's family used to own a small restaurant chain in Florida, and I guess he grew up with some money. For some reason his dad bought a ranch in Montana years ago but never went there. Probably used it as a tax shelter or something. Then he died and left it to Iggy. It's not a working ranch. No one lives there. Apparently, it's a big farmhouse and a few hundred acres. We've been invited up – there's a sledding hill. I told him to let me know next time he heads up there." Josie took a bite of the sandwich.

"Sounds like he lived the good life on his parent's money and when his wife figured out the money was gone she split. Iggy told me he spent his inheritance trying to make her happy, only to have her leave him for a college professor." Josie glanced at her phone to check the time.

"What does he do besides party and ski? Does he have a job?" Alice finished her sandwich and took a sip of coffee.

"He owns a graphic design business. Lark Creek Graphics. He doesn't seem to work very hard, though. He always seems to have time to head up skiing whenever there's fresh powder."

"Yeah, I know the type. He's just one more Montana trustifarian. A trust fund baby. This town is full of them. Pretty much every ski town and college town in the Rocky Mountains has their own little group of trust-funders. They usually have some little business, or maybe they set up a non-profit that spends ninety percent of the money they collect on their own salary," Alice said with disdain.

"You may be right Alice. Good for him. I wouldn't turn down a trust fund - in fact I plan on coming back as a trust-funder in my next life." Josie pushed back her chair and put on her hat and gloves.

"I'm making lasagna tonight – why don't you come over for dinner and then we can get to the legal stuff afterwards." She stood up.

"Sounds like a plan," Alice agreed, following Josie out the door.

❧ 36 ❧

Josie sorted the legal papers by date and laid them out on the dining room table. Phoebe sat quietly in the living room doing homework while Austen ran around the apartment shrieking as the puppy pulled his socks off and tossed them in the air.

"First things first," Alice said, getting down to business. "Do you know how to check the docket?" Alice had set her up her computer on the dining room table and Josie sat down beside her.

"Nope," Josie replied, shaking her head. "I don't know the first thing about this."

Alice typed in the words 'La Costa County family court' and the website came up. She clicked on a link, and typed in Josie's name. "Here it is. Here's your docket, Josie. You need to bookmark this and check it daily. Maybe even twice a day." Alice scrolled down the page.

"Looks like you have a court date coming up next month. Did you know that?" Alice asked. Josie shook her head 'no'.

"It's a hearing. Something about custody and child support. There's also something about the property settlement. They want you to check in and tell them where you are on it."

"We're nowhere, of course. Richard won't settle. He'll drag me through a trial. He already told me what his plan is when he came up here last month." Josie got up to check on the kids and quietly closed the French doors that separated the living room and dining room.

Alice picked up one of the legal papers and flipped through several pages. "This looks like a motion. Request for order. Proof of service. Responsive declaration," Alice read the legal terms out loud.

"But something isn't right," she continued. "When I went to court up here in Montana, the first page was stamped with a date. There's supposed to be something showing that it's been filed with the court. See Josie, the way it works is you fill out the legal papers, and then you bring them to the courthouse and go to the clerk's window. Usually you pay a fee, and then the court takes the paperwork and stamps it. You need to have a copy for the court, a copy for Weiner and a copy for yourself," Alice paused. "This document doesn't have a stamp on it. The court never stamped it so, as far as I can tell it's never been filed."

Alice put the document down and started opening more envelopes. One by one, she took legal papers out of their envelopes and flipped through them.

"Not one of these things has been filed, Josie. Not one." Alice motioned to a stack of over a dozen envelopes.

"What does that mean?" Josie asked hesitantly.

"It means you don't have to do anything about any of them. It's a smokescreen. It's a barrage of legal paperwork that's purely meant to intimidate you. What a slime ball that guy is. There are probably ethics rules against stuff like this, but of course Weiner doesn't follow them."

"But then, that's good news isn't it?" Josie brightened.

"Yes, it's good news but it's also pure bullying and intimidation. And let's face it, it worked. It put you into a three-week state of despondency. I was really worried about you. The only reason I didn't call the police and have them check on you was that I'm friends with Phoebe's teacher, and I asked her to let me know if she noticed Phoebe absent for any length of time. Otherwise I would have had them do a welfare check on you."

"Thanks Alice. I had a few rough days." Josie lowered her voice. "You know I saved an entire bottle of pain meds the hospital sent me home with after Austen was born. I never used them but for some reason, without even thinking about it, I never threw that bottle of pills away." Alice stopped what she was doing and looked at her friend.

"So, one night about a week ago I got the bottle out of the cabinet and just sat on the floor in my bathroom and sobbed. I was in the worst pain ever. I just couldn't process how this all ended up happening to me. I felt like my life was hijacked. The pain was so bad and I had that bottle of pain meds in my hand. An entire bottle…" Josie paused and shook her head.

"So what did you do?" Alice asked.

"I cried for a long time, but eventually I flushed the pills down the toilet. I was afraid of them. I was afraid of what I might do. And to tell you the truth I'm still trying to figure out why I hung on to them in the first place."

"That's a relief, Josie." Alice reached for Josie's hand. "I'm glad you got rid of that stuff. Call me anytime if you need to go out for a beer and talk. I can even get some smoke if you think that would help," she offered.

"Anyway, this tsunami of fake litigation was all calculated to demoralize you and destroy you. Weiner knows you have no legal training and you're out of money to pay the lawyer. He figured a daily visit from the express mail truck would have the desired effect. You can bet he does this to every pro-per litigant."

"I didn't tell you, but last month Weiner called me," Josie said. "It was right after I took over my own case. I picked up the phone and heard his voice. So smarmy and self satisfied." Josie shivered. "I felt sick just hearing hm. He said something about sending me a settlement agreement to sign. I asked him to just tell me what their offer was. Basically, it boiled down to Richard keeps the house in Loranda and half my retirement and one of my properties that I bought years before we met and I get to keep the rest. I asked if that meant he wasn't going to take me back to court for custody again and he said the settlement offer had nothing to do with custody. Anyway, I told him no thanks and hung up. The following weekend Richard came up to visit the kids. After he put the kids in the car he told me that he'd never settle and we were going to go to trial. It was right after that that the mailings started coming every day."

"Tell me something I don't already know, Josie," Alice said. "Of course he's going to take this to trial. You'll be lucky just to keep the properties you had when you met him. The sooner you forget about getting any of the marital property the better," Alice said harshly.

"So I'm a pro-per now." Josie changed the subject.

"It just means you're acting as your own lawyer. I don't know what the words actually mean."

Josie went into the kitchen to make tea and Alice followed. "It does make me angry to think that I let myself get depressed over all this stuff and then most of it turns out to be nothing. What a dick." She looked around to see if either of the kids was within earshot.

The two women took their tea cups and sat back down to work. Alice picked up another envelope and tore it open. "This was filed two weeks ago." She showed Josie the stamp. "A hearing is set for next month. Something about custody, child support and having you pay for the kid's health insurance." Alice read through the document carefully.

"He has a full time job that includes health insurance. He barely pays anything for it. I don't even have a job – how am I supposed to afford insurance?" Josie protested.

"You do what everyone else up here does that doesn't have insurance – you sign up for a class at the university. Once you're a student you can buy student insurance for yourself and the kids. I know plenty of people who do it. The insurance is kind of sucky, but it's better than nothing," Alice said.

Alice tore open another envelope and started reading, as Josie sipped her tea. "Okay, this looks like a declaration, and it's also been filed. Who's Kathy?" Alice handed the papers to Josie.

"That's Richard's sister." Josie flipped through the papers. "So now his family is piling on too? She's trashing me and saying I'm a terrible mother? Wow. Of course she knows nothing about raising kids because she and her husband never bothered to have any!" Josie angrily threw the papers down on the table. "Unbelievable."

"Here's another one." Alice handed Josie another filing. "Okay, great. This one is from one of the neighbors across the street from us in Loranda. She's in her seventies and her kids are grown. Richard used to go over there and hang out with her husband and watch the game. Geez, I can't believe she signed an affidavit trying to make me look bad. And it's totally lame anyway. She says I must be a bad mother because she never sees the kids playing in the front of the house." Josie put the paper down and stood up. "This is really unbelievable! Our house didn't even have a front yard! There's a tiny patch of grass and a steep concrete driveway. The kids played in the backyard. And to think I was always so nice to her. I used to bring her figs and berries from our garden." Josie sat down again, frowning.

"None of the rest of these has been filed," Alice said. "Weiner just wants to bury you - or at least make you think he's buried you, so if you do manage to come up for air you'll grab whatever they offer you." Alice got up and poured herself more tea.

"Look, Josie. I've given your situation a lot of thought. Richard is willing to have a nuclear war against you to get that property. I have no doubt he'll spend more than the property is even worth just to get it. He'll step over a dollar to pick up a dime just to hurt you." Alice paused.

"Tim says the person with the best lawyer usually wins and the person with no lawyer is almost guaranteed to lose."

"I know, Alice. That's why I'm so demoralized. I think that's why I was so depressed since Austen was born. When I lost my career, I lost any leverage I had in the marriage and deep down I think I knew Richard would take advantage of that. We went to marriage counseling for a few weeks and he proposed that he take Austen and I take Phoebe and we just go our separate ways. The therapist just sat there shaking his head."

Alice began to pace the room, thinking out loud. "Once you have the right mind-set everything will be okay – trust me, Josie. You'll be fine and the kids will be fine. Here's what I'm thinking. The main thing is the welfare of the kids – giving them a happy childhood. Do you agree?"

"Yes, of course," Josie said

"Can you live on the income from your rental properties until you get squared away with a new career?"

"Yes, I think so. If I had to," Josie said.

"Then the goal is not to get a just and equitable settlement. That isn't going to happen. We have to redefine the goal. The goal is to give the kids a happy childhood and to focus on a new career for yourself. Write off the house in Loranda and all the furniture. Half of your IRA is his and none of his IRA is yours. Get over trying to hang on to any of it. The less you have to lose the stronger you'll be – the more power you'll have in this process. The person with nothing left to lose is the most dangerous of all." Alice stopped pacing and looked at Josie.

"So, that brings me to my main point." Alice started pacing again.

"This problem is bigger than you. I see your real agenda as doing everything in your power to change this corrupt, money driven system. You need to fight them on their terms. Weiner papered your house with motions and declarations – you need to do the same to them. You need to start filing declarations. You need to file motions. Every time you sit down to write, you need to tell the truth about the abuse you and the kids endured and how venal and corrupt the system is that has enabled Richard and Weiner to do what they do. Don't hold back, Josie. You're going to lose anyway so you need to bash in as many kneecaps as you can on your way down," Alice said, relishing the prospect.

"I'm scared, Alice. You're talking about lawyers and judges. These are powerful people. And then there's the Bain family with all their millions. I can't really do what you're describing," Josie said.

Alice leaned over and put both hands on the table. "Okay, what's the worst that can happen? Unless you directly threaten someone, everything you write is protected speech. It's a foregone conclusion that the property settlement is a total joke. You won't get anything, so write it off. The kids are protected. I don't doubt for a minute that Richard will take you back to court to get them – but guess what? He'll fail. Unless you develop a drinking problem or a drug habit or the kids find you having sex on the dining room table when they walk in the front door after school – there really isn't anything that can happen to you."

"That's not true, Alice. People think the mom always gets custody no matter what, but it isn't true. I had to fight to get custody and part of the reason I got it was that Richard screwed up so badly. And now he's getting remarried and from everything I've read it's really true – a lot of judges will favor a married couple over a single mom. In fact, I feel like a pariah now that I'm a single mom. We're responsible for every bad thing that happens in society – haven't you noticed? Anyway, the lawyer specifically told me that custody can change anytime. Whenever the situation changes, the custody can change. It's called a change of circumstance. As soon as Richard gets re-married, bam – he'll take me back to court and there's a good chance he'll win!"

Alice sat down across from Josie. "Okay, so technically it may be true that custody can change anytime. Didn't you tell me that the court likes stability for kids? They've already been yanked out of their home in California and they're doing well up here – I think you can make a strong case for keeping them here just because they need stability. I think now that you have primary custody the game is yours to lose. From what I've seen since you moved back here, you don't do anything that could get you in trouble. You won't even meet me at Zippy's for a beer," Alice said.

"So, I give up on the house and the furniture and my IRA, because it's a foregone conclusion that he's going to win," Josie started writing on a yellow pad. "I don't worry about custody, because I've already passed one evaluation with flying colors and the court wants stability for the kids. Can't I still get in trouble somehow? Technically, can't the judge throw me in jail for going rouge and saying what really happened to me?" Josie asked.

"As long as you follow the orders of the court, there isn't much they can do to you. Of course don't ever threaten anyone. You'll hang on to most of what you had when you met him and you'll have primary custody of the kids and just kiss the rest of it goodbye. The time has come to fight back. You need to come out swinging. I say you write and write and write some more. You could write declarations and motions every day for the next month and you still wouldn't be caught up with this pile of stuff Weiner's already put out." Alice gestured at the pile of envelopes before them.

"Of course, the courts love to complain about litigants who they claim waste the courts time blah, blah, blah. The way I see it, if they're so upset then they need to change the way the courts work. They need to make the system fair. And you need to fight back with the only thing you have, Josie. Use your words. Start writing. Send me everything you write and I'll have Tim look it over for accuracy and let you know what he says. He wants to stay in the background but he's happy to help with legal advice."

∽ 37 ∾

"Come in!" Iggy called out from the kitchen. Josie stepped into the gloom of Iggy's cramped, subterranean apartment. There was a hint of disdain on her face as she glanced around at the motley assemblage that constituted his belongings.

"I found most of the furniture in the alley during semester break," Iggy said as he walked over to greet her, wiping his hands with a dish towel.

"No need to buy furniture in this town. I used to have some nice stuff, but I gave it all to Paul's mom," he said, noticing Josie's expression. A worn floral loveseat was pushed into the corner opposite the door, and a vinyl desk chair sat next to the small front window.

"Hey, Iggy, whatever works." Josie shrugged and followed Iggy into the galley-sized kitchen where he had been frying fish fillets in a small cast-iron pan.

"So, I guess the bright yellow paint job is supposed to make up for how dark it is in here." She squeezed past Iggy and sat down on an elaborately carved three-legged stool in the corner of the kitchen.

Iggy noticed her admiring the stool as she ran her fingers over the smooth dark wood.

"I got that in Africa years ago," Iggy told her.

"I lived on my boat for ten years and spent a lot of time over there. Somalia, Kenya. I was friends with all the pirates." He glanced at her to see her reaction.

"Really? That's interesting. I spent time at sea also. I got my engineering degree at the merchant marine academy and worked for a shipping company for a few years. Mostly in Asia. So what were you doing on a sail boat in Africa? We used to see small boats out at sea occasionally. It takes guts to go out there on a small boat. I went through a bad storm once on a super tanker and was scared shitless. We limped into the nearest shipyard after it was finally over. The repairs took weeks. It tore the ship apart."

Iggy pinched some salt between his fingers and sprinkled it on the fish before flipping the fillets.

"I always thought if I did go to sea in a small boat I'd get the fastest boat with the best navigational equipment I could afford," Josie continued. "That way I could see what was coming and outrun the storm."

"Well, you can forget that idea, Josie. You can't outrun the storm. I always tell people that I'm not the greatest sailor, but I'm the best there is when it comes to storm management. I take down the sails, stow everything and wait it out. When the weather clears I go topside and get my bearings. I've been blown hundreds of miles off course – but I always survived in good shape." Iggy smiled and handed Josie a plate of food.

Josie slowly ate her food as she stared blankly out the window. Traumatic memories of her time at sea came flooding back to her. It was over fifteen years earlier. She was in the engine room of a super tanker and things were starting to get rough. Never one to get sea-sick, she nevertheless began to feel waves of nausea wash over her. Tension filled the air as she and her watch partner exchanged nervous glances. Then the alarms started.

One by one, the salinity alarms went off – signaling that salty water had entered the pipes which lead back to the ship's boiler. Allowing salt water into the boiler is one of the worst things that can happen to a steam ship. Josie had always heard that salting the boilers meant having to scrap the entire ship. She'd once been told about a Japanese engineer who'd committed hara-kiri because he's allowed salt water to get into the boilers during his watch. Josie felt panic rising in her throat as she ran over to check the alarms.

"We need to dump all these lines! There's salt water coming back to the engine room! Quick, we need to find the valves and dump everything to the bilge. Something must have happened out on deck!" She yelled orders at her watch partner as they frantically located all the steam pipes coming back into the engine room and started opening valves that lead to the bilge. Her watch partner spoke up. Clean-cut and earnest, Josie was glad to have him with her during this crisis.

"I need to go topside. I have to find out where this is coming from and shut the valves at the source. Otherwise the bilge pumps won't be able to keep up," he told Josie as he went to find his foul weather gear.

"No – it's not safe!" Josie yelled over the roar of the turbines. "Really, you can't go – there's green water over the bow – I heard one of the boatswain's talking before I came on watch. Nobody is allowed on deck!" She followed him as he put on his gear and started climbing out of the engine room.

"We don't have a choice, Josie!" He yelled at her. "This is an emergency! The bilge pumps can't keep up and we can't salt the boilers!"

"Okay – you're right. But wait – I think we can rig up a tether and you can strap yourself to the railing when you get out there – it's better than nothing." The two engineers found an assortment of straps and clips for him to use.

"Wish me luck!" He yelled as he opened the hatch and exited the engine room. Josie fastened the hatch behind him and ran down several levels of ladders. Her arms were full of straps and fasteners and she stopped to wrap them around the tanks of welding gas. *If one of these came loose it would turn into a missile and we'd all be toast*, she thought as she wrapped straps around them.

Every engine room has a panic button, and for the first time in her career Josie had decided to use it. Before she could get to it though, she heard voices and looked behind her. The entire engineering staff was headed down to help – they'd been woken by the storm and instinctively knew to check the engine room.

Everyone worked together to get the engine room back to normal and Josie was relieved when her watch partner came back safe but shivering violently and as white as a sheet. He'd found the source of the problem - a several-hundred-pound steam winch that had been welded to the deck had broken off and been carried away by the heavy seas, leaving the steam pipes open to the salt water.

When her watch was finally over, she headed back up to her stateroom to sleep. It was four o'clock in the morning and she was exhausted. She belted herself into her bunk, as she'd been instructed to do during storms, and fell into a fitful sleep. In the middle of a nightmare about trying to escape from a sinking ship, Josie was woken by a loud bang. She jumped out of her bunk and went to investigate.

The chief engineer was in his office, struggling to remove a heavy steel safe from where it had lodged in the bulkhead. It had been welded to the deck and had broken loose due to the violent motion of the ship.

"I've been sailing for forty years and this is the worst captain I've ever worked with." The chief was a man of few words, and Josie was surprised that he was confiding in her.

"He was passed over for promotion several times and then they finally decided to give him a go. He saw the storm on his instruments but he's dead set on making his ETA. Most skippers would have changed course, but not this guy."

"Can't you say something Chief? You have so much more experience," Josie offered.

"No, I can't." The chief shrugged. "The skipper pulls rank on me. I've wrung more salt water out of socks than this guy has ever sailed over, but he's in charge." The chief shook his head sadly as he and Josie pried the heavy safe out of the bulkhead and tied it down.

"Wow, so he's too rigid to change course just because he wants to make his ETA. He's putting the ship and the entire crew at risk," Josie said. She lurched down the passageway and stepped into the mess-deck just as a jar of peanut butter flew across the compartment and smashed into a bulkhead.

Josie slowly chewed her food as she thought about that long-ago storm. "Earth to Josie – do you want to sit at the table and eat or just keep staring out the window?" Iggy asked impatiently.

"Uh, sorry, Iggy. I was just thinking. Actually I think you just helped me out with something." Josie stood and walked over to the small table.

"Really? How did I do that?" Iggy asked.

"What you said about not being able to outrun the storm. That you won't see it coming and you just have to practice storm management. It made me think about some stuff."

Iggy filled three small wooden dishes with food.

"By the way, did you feed the boys lunch today?" Josie asked between bites of fish and potatoes.

"Yep. I fed them. They're fine. And stop with the mother hen thing, Josie. You'll ruin that kid."

"All I want to know is if my kid ate anything today, and what you guys had. Geez. That's not mother hen. That's just…"

"Micro-managing," Iggy finished her sentence. "They're good. They're playing in Paul's room." Iggy walked out of the kitchen.

"Hey boys come out here! Dinner's ready! Austen's mom is here!" Iggy called out.

Austen appeared in the small living room and ran up to hug his mom. "Hi sweetie. Did you have a fun play-date?" She asked

"Jesus, Josie, how many times do I have to tell you not to say the word 'play-date,'" Iggy cringed.

"Yeah, Mom, it's not a play-date. It's just two guys hanging out," Austen informed her with a serious look on his face.

"Tell your mom what you guys had for lunch," Iggy urged him.

"Whiskey and cigarettes, whiskey and cigarettes!" Paul chimed in.

"Really?" Josie took Austen's chin in her hands. "Really? Whiskey and cigarettes?" Austen looked at his friend and nodded in agreement.

"Actually, I gave them both some elk jerky. Austen loved it. I make it myself. Every year I bag an elk on my ranch. It's the real reason I can't wait for the last day of hunting season." Iggy handed each of the boys a small wooden plate filled with fish and potatoes.

"Why can't you wait until the last day of hunting season? Most hunters go out on the first day of hunting season." Josie put her plate in the sink and walked back into the living room.

"The last day of hunting season means it's almost the first day of poaching season. Are you kidding me? I never go out when all those yahoos are out there shooting at each other." Iggy shrugged and sat down on the couch. He turned on the TV.

"My ranch, my rules. Nobody bothers me out there."

"Yeah right, Iggy. Poachers get caught all the time. You just haven't been caught yet. Anyway, thanks again for watching Austen this afternoon. And thanks for dinner, it was good." Josie took Austen by the hand and left.

∞ 38 ∞

"I think my neighbor is right." Josie was sitting on her front porch talking on the phone. It was early spring, and everything west of the Continental Divide, including Josie's hometown, was starting to bloom. The fruit trees were budding, and a few spindly tulip stems were poking through the fresh fertilizer in Josie's flower beds.

"Which neighbor? The crazy guy with the wild hair I met when I was up there? The guy who walks into your house without being invited? That guy?" Back home in California, Valerie was laying on her recliner in front of the muted TV.

"Yes Mom, the guy with the curly blond hair, Iggy. He sailed around on a small boat for years. We were talking about boats and he said something that really hit me. He told me that nobody can outrun a storm at sea, especially on a small boat. For some reason, it made me start thinking about my life, and my predicament with Richard. Iggy told me that the key to survival is good storm management," Josie paused.

"I guess I just suddenly saw the truth of it. I always figured I would see trouble heading my way and out-maneuver it. Obviously, I was wrong. Sometimes you don't see the trouble coming, and you don't have time to get out of the way. I just keep thinking about what I should have done – even though I know it's a waste of time because I can't change the past. What I really need to focus on right now is storm management." Josie walked around to the side of the house where the lilacs were starting to bloom.

"I started to tell Iggy about the one really bad storm that happened when I sailed on an oil tanker years ago. Remember, Mom? I know I told you and Dad about it. The captain was a total jerk and he'd been passed over for promotion several times. Then right when I was assigned to the ship they decided to finally promote him to skipper," Josie paused.

"I think I remember hearing about that guy, Josie. He lived in Marin County, right?" Valerie said as she watched the muted TV.

"Yeah, I forget his name – but that's him. So anyway, we got into this bad storm and this guy was in charge of the ship. And because he'd been passed over a bunch of times he had something to prove. Most captains would change course when they see a storm coming, even if it means being delayed. It's more important to protect the ship and the crew than it is to make the ETA. Not this guy though. He decided to sail right straight through it. He thought he'd impress the company by making his ETA, no matter what. He was totally rigid and he refused to change course. The chief engineer had been sailing for decades – he told me this was the worst captain he'd ever sailed with. I was down in the engine room and it was really rough. Suddenly all the alarms went off at the same time. I found out later that a steam winch had been torn off the deck and that sea water went into the pipes straight into the engine room. The whole watch was a nightmare. My watch partner risked his life and probably saved all of us. When I finally got to my room I had to tie myself into my bunk so I wouldn't be thrown out. After it was finally over we limped into the nearest shipyard."

"I remember the story, Josie. It's stuff like that that made your dad and I so worried about you," Valerie said.

"Well anyway, it's been years since I've thought about that ship, but talking to Iggy made me realize that now I'm the one who's acting stupid. I'm acting like that skipper."

"How so?" Valerie asked.

"Because I can't let go of everything I've worked so hard for – like being able to put my kids through college and have a nice retirement someday. It's like I want to make my ETA no matter what but I can't and it's tearing me up. Thinking I can somehow stay the course is just causing me a lot of anguish, when really I just need to accept the fact that I didn't see the storm coming and I've been blown way off course. That captain couldn't accept it and ended up wrecking the ship and putting all of our lives at risk. Do you see, Mom?" Josie asked.

"You're talking about crisis management, Josephine – but I think you need to give yourself more credit. It seems to me that you've done marvelously well so far. You protected the kids. You got the move-away, and your lawyer told you nobody ever gets that. The move went smoothly, you've made new friends already, and the kids have adjusted well. It's not what happens to us in life; it's how we deal with it that matters. As far as I can see, you've played the cards you were dealt and you're holding your own." Valerie picked up the remote and silently flipped through the channels.

"It may look like that on the outside, Mom, but that's just my game face. Deep down inside I can't seem to accept the fact that I have to change course. I still think I should have the big house in California and the good paying job and a great retirement and pay for my kid's college. In fact, I have to do what Iggy did on his sailboat. Just get down to bare essentials. Forget about making headway and accept the fact that you're going to be blown off course. I need to be more flexible."

"So what does all that mean to you?" Valerie asked.

"It means I have to reevaluate everything. I love Montana, but I never thought I'd end up back here. In some ways it feels like failure – I left when I was seventeen to make my fortune, only to come crawling back over twenty years later as a single mother. I won't be resuming my engineering career, either – we all know there are no jobs up here. I'm going to have to rely on my rental property income a lot more than I ever thought I would. It means I have to get creative. Sometimes, I think I can't even take my survival for granted."

"Wow, Josie. That's a little ominous." Valerie was alarmed.

"I know, Mom. I haven't called much lately because I've been battling a pretty bad depression. A neighbor of mine just committed suicide last week. She tried to be my new best friend when I first moved in, but I just couldn't deal with her problems at the time. I could barely deal with my own."

"Is that the tall dark-haired woman with the daughter Phoebe's age?" Valerie suddenly sat straight up, stunned to hear about the suicide.

"Yes, that's her. Tall, super skinny, talked non-stop," Josie concurred.

"I thought she was unstable the one time I met her. In fact, I remember telling you I thought she was on something," Valerie said.

"I don't know if she was on something, I just thought she was a mess. She was going through a divorce. I met her down at the bus stop one morning with the kids and invited her in for coffee, remember? The one time she came over, she sat on my couch and cried. Her husband had left her for someone else. I felt bad for her, but I just couldn't deal with her. Her kid stopped taking the bus right after that, and I figured they'd moved away. Then last week I was unloading groceries from my car and Iggy walked up and told me the news. The ambulance had just left with her body. Apparently, she got into the bathtub and took a bunch of pills. She texted her husband and I guess he came over and found her." Josie shuddered.

"That's awful. Oh my God." Valerie turned off the TV.

"And the weirdest thing is that her daughter was at our house later, playing with my kids as if nothing had happened. Everyone in the neighborhood knows about it. Even though I really didn't know her, I think hearing about her suicide triggered my own depression. It sort of comes and goes. Right now I'm feeling okay. I'm in the garden and the sun is out. The trees are starting to green. Anyway, I have to go. I'll call again later."

Josie hung up the phone and walked around the yard. Years ago when she first bought the building she and her father had planted fruit trees and berry bushes along the front and side yards. The apple tree was still there, as were the cherry and the peach. The blueberries were barely hanging on, but the cranberry bushes were massive.

It was April, and the ground was starting to thaw. The snow had melted, and Josie could see bare spots where the lawn had died. She bent over and felt the ground before lying down on her stomach, between the fruit trees. She spread her arms wide and pressed her body into the earth.

She'd read once that if she ever felt ungrounded she should lie down on the ground and embrace the earth with her arms wide open. She'd thought it was hokey and new-agey at the time. Now she no longer cared about what others might think so she tried it, and it felt good. The sun warmed her back, and the ground was solid and cool beneath her. She turned her face towards the house, closed her eyes and fell asleep.

A bald eagle perched on a gnarled stump next to Josie's house. He let out a piercing scream and lifted his wings to fly. Soaring effortlessly through the open front door, he swooped and dived through the rooms. With one or two flaps he soared from one end of Josie's apartment to the other, banking and turning when he reached a wall. After circling through the apartment, he came to rest on the kitchen counter. He spread his wings wide, and began flapping vigorously. He flapped dozens of times, each time sending strong currents of air pulsating through the house. All the windows blew open as the eagle continued to flap. Dark sooty air billowed from the windows, and dissipated in the breeze. Then, the eagle took off and glided through the house again. He landed once more, and this time each flap of his wings drew a rush of clear blue air into the house. As the house filled up with fresh air, the eagle soared back through the open door and all the windows fell back into place.

Josie awoke after her brief nap, sat up and stretched. She was renewed and refreshed. She entered the apartment and without thinking went room to room, parting drapes, pulling up shades and opening windows. Fresh air and sunlight flooded into every room. The gloom that had settled on Josie and had filled her home and her heart with darkness for the last few weeks had finally lifted. She plugged in the old boom box she'd found in one of the closets – abandoned by a previous tenant along with a stack of banged up CDs. Putting in a random disk and turning up the volume, she found herself singing and dancing to the tune of an old 1970s rock group. She was happy, calm and free.

⚸ 39 ⚸

The children watched as Josie hung yellow caution tape across the bathroom door. "Don't use it and make sure none of your friends uses it, either!" She shook her finger at the kids. "It's strictly off limits! No exceptions!" Phoebe, Austen and Paul nodded dutifully before running back outside.

The judge had finally agreed to let Josie make her next court appearance by phone, and she'd focused all her energy on getting ready for that. She'd flown back to California the first time acting as her own attorney, only to have the hearing postponed at the last minute. Now the hearing was coming up again and it was clear there was a major plumbing problem in the one of her bathrooms.

The plumber stood in the dimly lit basement and used his flashlight to point to the corner of one of the walls. "The leak is back there, behind this wall." He slapped the ancient plaster with his hand.

"I can't get at it from here. It's too tight. We're going to have to cut a hole in the bathroom floor and climb down. I don't know what we'll find, but based on the age of this place, the sewer line is probably worn out and needs replacing." He shut off the flashlight and turned to Josie.

"Well, great. Just great," Josie said, shaking her head in dismay. "It is what it is, I guess. Go ahead and do whatever you need to do. I assume it would be okay to use the other bathroom in the meantime?"

"Yes ma'am, back then everything was plumbed in separate. Go ahead and use the other bathroom for now." He headed up the basement stairs as Josie followed behind.

"I really need at least a ballpark estimate of what this will cost, though," Josie called out to the plumber as she ducked under the yellow tape and followed him into the bathroom.

"Hard to say until I've seen it," the plumber replied. "You'll also need to call one of those cleanup crews that can pump out all the sewage in the basement. Those guys aren't cheap either. I have a card in my van I'll give you." With his thin build and long limbs, Josie had been hoping that the plumber would be able to squeeze behind the wall in the basement and prevent having to tear up the bathroom. No such luck.

"I'll need to cut a hole right here – about two feet square." The plumber motioned to the bathroom floor. "Once the cleanup guys get done, we'll air it out for a couple days and then I'll go down and start working."

"Okay, so when can you get started?" Josie tapped her foot anxiously. The plumber took out his phone and slowly scrolled through his appointments.

"I'm busy all next week, but I have time tomorrow. I'll cut the hole and take some measurements. I'll order the fixtures. You'll need a new toilet, maybe a sink," he said as he measured the space with his metal tape. "You can arrange to have the cleanup guys here at the same time so they can get started right away. Then I'll come back and get to work."

"Tomorrow? That's a really bad day for me. I'm going through a divorce in California and I actually have a phone hearing tomorrow. It's an actual court hearing here in my house - by phone. It has to be totally quiet with no distractions."

"Well, it's either that or we wait another two weeks." The plumber shrugged. "But I don't recommend waiting. As the owner of this building you could be in trouble if the tenants find out there's raw sewage in the basement and you're not taking care of it."

"I've been there too, by the way. Been divorced twice, and believe me it's no fun."

"Twice? Really? What are you twenty-five?" Josie looked at the plumber, astounded.

"Okay, fine," Josie sighed. "It looks like it's going to have to be tomorrow. Also, can you call that cleanup crew and have everyone here first thing? Like at eight? You know the guy, right? Maybe everything can be done by the time my hearing starts at ten."

The next morning a large white truck fitted with a cylindrical tank parked in the alley behind Josie's house. Gray rubber hoses snaked across the backyard, through an open window and disappeared down the roughly cut hole in the bathroom floor. Josie sat down at the dining room table and briefly closed her eyes to compose herself. She tried to block out the drone of the sewage pump and the voices of the contractors. She envisioned herself performing at the hearing, answering all the questions professionally, making all the right remarks and scoring points with the judge. Even though she was alone in her dining room in Montana, she had dressed for the part. She'd put on her court outfit – her light gray suit with the slightly flared skirt and a white blouse, along with some light makeup. Her hair was twisted into a bun and all the legal papers for the hearing were neatly organized on the table before her.

The phone rang and Josie opened her eyes, startled. It was ten minutes before the hearing was supposed to start. She answered. A man from the court told her to stand by, and then the clerk's voice came on the line. The clerk asked her to state her name and informed Josie that she was now in the courtroom. Josie nervously walked over and opened the dining room doors again to check that her 'do not disturb' sign was in place. She closed the doors and pulled them tight.

"Okay thanks," she told the clerk. Outside, she heard the contractors yelling to each other.

"I think the hose is blocked!" One of the contractors yelled over the sound of the pump.

"I'll go downstairs and check it out!" The other one yelled back.

Josie heard the pumps shut down and watched through the dining room window as one of the men walked along the side yard and up on to her front porch.

"Mrs. Bain we are ready for you to join the session." Josie heard the clerk say on the other end of the line. "Remember that court is in session and there is to be no unnecessary noise. No talking, no TV, no cell phone," she informed Josie.

"Yes ma'am," Josie replied, trying to speak clearly and calmly while at the same time realizing that she'd forgotten to put a 'do not disturb' sign on the front door.

"Mrs. Bain this is Judge Shumacher. Are you there?" Just then the doorbell rang.

"Yes, Your Honor. I'm here." Josie cupped her hand over the phone to block the sound of the doorbell. She ran out of the dining room as quietly and quickly as she could, and pulled back the living room drapes. Tapping on the window she gestured frantically to the contractor who was standing in front of her door with his finger on the buzzer. The man looked up and Josie pointed to the phone and shook her head vigorously side-to-side, silently voicing "no."

The man shrugged and pointed towards the backyard. "We're having trouble with the pump," he shouted through the closed window. "We need to get into the basement."

Josie frantically nodded yes and pointed towards the side door while she ran through the house to let the contractors into the basement.

"Mr. Bain is here with his attorney, and Mrs. Bain is here by phone from Montana." The judge continued talking as Josie unlocked the side door and silently motioned the workers towards the basement stairs. "We're here on the child support and visitation matter. Mr. Bain has asked the court to order a new custody evaluation due to a change in circumstances. Mrs. Bain, are you still with us? What's that noise?" The judge asked.

Josie raced back in the dining room and quickly closed the doors behind her. "Yes, Your Honor. I'm still here. Do you want me to talk now?" She asked.

"No, Mrs. Bain. Mr. Bain brought the motion so he will go first."

"Adam Weiner here, representing Richard Bain." Josie cringed at the sound of Weiner's voice. *Smarmy asshole*, she thought to herself.

"We brought this motion because my client has been over-paying his child support, and because he wants more visitation time with the children. He is also remarried and asks the court to order a new custody evaluation in light of his changed circumstances." Josie smoothed her skirt and quietly sat down at the table, trying to collect her thoughts. She nervously leafed through the legal papers in front of her, and tried to focus on the proceedings. Loud footsteps pounded up and down the basement stairs and in the hallway outside the dining room door.

"Mrs. Bain has now been in Montana for four months and still has not found suitable employment. We ask the court to order her to find employment and to seek out a career counselor."

As usual during court proceedings, Josie felt like retching. She'd agreed not to ask for spousal support because she thought it meant that Richard wouldn't have anything to say about her employment situation. She'd had enough to do trying to get settled and she already knew how notoriously difficult it was to find a job in an isolated college town.

"What do you have to say about that, Mrs. Bain?" The judge asked.

"Your Honor, this is the third time in less than a year that Mr. Bain has gone to court to lower his child support. It has also been less than a year since our custody evaluation. Mr. Bain refuses to make a property settlement with me, and has stated that he'll take me to trial on the matter. I will have to return to school for a graduate degree in order to find suitable employment where I live, and I am waiting for my property settlement to pay for school." Josie finished speaking. She continued to cup her hand over the phone to block the sound of the contractor's voices just outside the door.

"Okay," the judge responded. "I am putting you under a seek-work order, Mrs. Bain. You are to begin reporting your work-seeking efforts at the start of next month. Mr. Weiner will supply you with the forms. You will report the time and date and contact information for at least four employers per week that you have sought employment with." The judge paused. "Do you understand, Mrs. Bain?"

Josie leaned her head on her hand. "Yes, Your Honor."

"I will also order an update on the custody evaluation and a recalculation of the child support," the judge continued.

"I have the child support calculations here, Your Honor," Weiner chimed in. Josie listened to the sound of rustling papers and muffled voices in the courtroom while the smell of raw sewage drifted into the dining room where she sat.

"Okay. Are you following this, Mrs. Bain?" The judge asked again. "Your child support is being reduced in accordance with the law, and you are required to seek work. I am also ordering a revised custody evaluation with Dr. Stokes, assuming he is available."

"Your Honor, can I speak again?" Josie sat up straight and tried to stay calm. "We've only been in Montana for about four months. The children are still adjusting to their new life. I think it is premature to have another custody evaluation so soon after the first one. Dr. Stokes himself said that the children need stability. I think they should have more time to get used to the custody situation as it is."

"Your Honor," Wiener interrupted. "My client is newly married and wants his children to be part of his new family. My client's new wife has been an excellent mother to her own children, and would like the chance to be a full time step-mother to her husband's children. As you know, Your Honor, all the studies have shown that children are better off with two parents, as opposed to being raised by a single mother such as Mrs. Bain. Mr. Bain is willing to be very generous with visitation. Further, since Mrs. Bain has family and friends in the Bay Area and Mr. Bain doesn't know anyone in Montana, it will be much less of a hardship for her to visit the children than it is for my client," Weiner continued.

Josie gasped audibly. "What do you have to say about that Mrs. Bain?" The judge asked.

"Your Honor, Mr. Bain didn't put any of that in his motion." Josie responded, trying not to raise her voice.

"That's what the hearing is for," the judge stated briskly.

"Well, Dr. Stokes said in his report that I am an excellent mother," Josie replied. "The children are thriving in Montana. There is no need for a new custody evaluation. I also want to say something about the seek-work order, Your Honor." Josie didn't stop to wait for a response from the judge. The contractors had started the pump back up and were standing in the hall just outside her door, talking loudly.

"Before I got sick during my last pregnancy, I made more money than Mr. Bain. I lost my license because he hid my renewal notice shortly after our son was born. The only reason he even has his current high-paying job is because I helped him get it. I live in an isolated college town in the Rocky Mountains, Your Honor. This is the worst recession we've had in generations. The only way to get a good paying job here, even in good times, is to have an advanced degree. Even then it's hard. I've put forth many good faith offers to Mr. Bain and he won't settle. He wants to take me to trial so he can bankrupt me. I can't begin graduate school until I have my settlement. I never asked for alimony and I just want him to do his fair share to help support our kids. His child support is less than ten percent of his take home pay. It doesn't even cover the expense of the visitation travel that Dr. Stokes ordered me to do. The whole reason this divorce happened is because he abused our children and I was ordered by the county social worker to protect them." Josie paused as she walked over to the window.

Suddenly, she heard Weiner speak up loudly. "I object, Your Honor. Mrs. Bain is once again repeating unfounded allegations of abuse against my client."

"Objection sustained. Strike Mrs. Bain's statement from the record," the judge said.

Josie immediately jumped back in. "Don't you see what's happening here, Your Honor? There isn't a level playing field in my case. Mr. Bain has endless funds from his family to keep litigating. He just wants me to give up and give him my property and the kids and everything. I'm an excellent mother. I have sacrificed everything to protect my kids and give them a good childhood. Mr. Bain is using up the court's precious time for his own selfish ends. He files motion after motion. I need equal justice in my case, Your Honor. Did you read my response declaration? I wrote everything I had to say in my filing..." As Josie paused to take a breath, the judge spoke.

"You've had your say Mrs. Bain," he said briskly.

"The seek-work order stands. I will set the property issue for trial. There is a new child support order effective immediately. Assuming Dr. Stokes is available, I am ordering the parties to pay for an updated custody evaluation." He banged his gavel.

Josie stood in her dining room with the phone to her ear. She stared blankly out the window as the color drained from her face. She suddenly felt ill. The men outside were still yelling, and the sewage pump was still droning, but she didn't hear any of it. She held on to the phone and listened to the muffled sounds of the courtroom a thousand miles away. Then she heard a dial tone and slumped back down into her chair.

⚮ 40 ⚮

Alice sat on the couch in Josie's living room reading a book to Austen, while Phoebe softly practiced the piano. Josie hustled around the house picking up books and backpacks and putting shoes away.

The doorbell rang. Without waiting for an answer, Paul ran in and headed straight back to Austen's room. Iggy came in after him and closed the door. Austen jumped off Alice's lap and ran into the back of the house calling after his best friend.

"The crack legal team is here, I see. Maybe you guys can help me out. After dinner we can park the kids in front of a movie and talk strategy." Josie was wearing an apron over her jeans and had one hand on her hip.

Iggy and Alice followed her into the kitchen. Iggy opened the refrigerator and found a beer, while Alice sat down at the table in the breakfast nook.

"Right now I'm down for the count. My last hearing was a disaster. The contractors were here working on the sewage problem, and I was in the dining room trying to focus on the hearing. When I got a chance to talk I tried to say everything I possibly could. I remembered Tim's advice – that if you assume the judge has read your filing you will lose. So I just tried to stuff everything I could think of into my statements – I didn't want to assume anything. Honestly I think it backfired." Josie took the lasagna out of the oven and got some plates down from the cupboard.

"He ruled against me on every single issue," Josie continued. "Now we're having another custody evaluation. He ordered a trial on the property issues. He lowered the child support again, and also ordered me to start reporting to Weiner about my quote 'job-seeking efforts.' It's so humiliating. If it wasn't for me, Richard wouldn't even have that job, and if it wasn't for him sabotaging my career I'd still be making good money." Josie sat down at the table next to Alice and put her head in her hands.

"Here, have a beer." Iggy handed Josie his unopened beer and reached in the fridge for another.

"Chillax, Josie. The judge plays tennis with Weiner – you told me that yourself. That's why Richard and his family picked Weiner. I told you from the beginning not to expect any fairness. It's not about that. Don't go in to these hearings with any big expectations. Your expectations are what kill you every time. It sets you up for a big letdown. Always assume the worst when you're dealing with our so-called justice system," Alice said, trying to console her friend.

"All my life I've been told we have the finest justice system in the world. What a joke," she continued. "The judge plays tennis with your opposing attorney and that's considered okay? Is this why my dad went to the Naval Academy and fought in two wars - to defend this?" Alice shook her head in dismay.

Iggy got another beer and slid it over to Alice. She twisted off the cap and took a sip.

"I know, Alice. I wonder the same things. I'm trying to manage my expectations. I keep telling myself not to expect anything. There is no justice when one party can outspend the other one a hundred times over. It's a corrupt, money-driven system. There is no level playing field. You get as much justice as you can afford, and these days I can't afford any. Like you always tell me Alice, the best I can do is bust a few kneecaps on my way down. Giving my kids an awesome childhood, rebuilding my life and doing my best to expose the corrupt family court system – that's my entire M.O," Josie said as she got up to finish making dinner.

"Remember you guys, it's not about gender," Iggy said, pulling up a chair. "Every guy I know thinks they get screwed in family court and women all think the same thing. It's about the money. It's always about the money. It's an incestuous system made up of lawyers and judges that often know each other and socialize together and some-times went to school together or practiced together. If your mother gave you a couple hundred thousand to litigate this and Richard's mother didn't, he'd be toast. Money talks, bullshit walks. You'd get everything – the house, the kids. You'd get to keep your entire pension because you would've seen an attorney early in the marriage and been given all the advice Richard got," Iggy said.

After dinner Josie cleared the dishes before putting the latest stack of legal mailings in the middle of the table. She set out three yellow pads and several pens and set up a white board on a small easel at the end of the oversized table. The boys were watching a movie in the next room and Phoebe was in her bedroom reading. Iggy's phone rang and he walked out of the room to answer it.

"Who's he talking to?" Alice asked, motioning to Iggy.

"Oh, it's probably his girl friend du jour. I can't keep track of them. I've only known him a few months and I think he's told me about four different women he's taken out. Or maybe it's something about the business. He's trying to get his graphic design business off the ground," Josie answered.

"Hey!" Iggy came back in the room. "Are you two talking about me? All I can say is that before my divorce I never realized there were so many hot single women out there. Women who wouldn't have looked twice at me in college and suddenly they're all over me. I'm a hot commodity around here," he boasted.

"Must be nice," Josie shrugged. "Anyway, let's get down to business. We have until the movie ends. Here, you guys can each open one of these things and we can all start reading. This part always makes me a nervous wreck." She handed an envelope to each of her friends.

"I'm just so grateful to you guys for helping me with this. I owe you. Just when I think it can't get any worse, it gets worse. It's the not knowing what the next thing is going to be that makes me feel like puking." Josie sat down and arranged her yellow pad next to her as she hesitated opening her envelope. A queasy feeling bubbled up in her stomach and throat.

Alice dumped out the contents of her envelope and started flipping through the pages. "It looks like a new child support motion. Geez, Josie is this true?" She looked across the table at her friend. "I work with guys that pay more than this for one kid, and they don't make anywhere near what Richard makes."

"Well, it's complicated, Alice. Even though I'm not working the court assumes I can make an engineer's wages and they count that as part of the equation – it's called imputation of income. It makes Richard's child support a lot lower that way. I told them about my license and everything and they couldn't care less." Josie had already adjusted to the lower child support and wasn't letting it bother her. She tore open her envelope and pulled out a pile of legal papers. "This must be the seek-work order." She flipped through several pages before tearing open another envelope. "This looks like another copy of the child support order." Josie slid the papers over to Alice.

"Yep. These two are identical." Alice confirmed. "What about you, Iggy – what do you have?"

Iggy's reading glasses had transformed him from a wild-haired ski bum into a professorial and urbane-looking guy. "So this is the order for the custody evaluation. Dr. Stoked," Iggy read out loud. "Ten thousand bucks. What a racket. I have to say, I'd be stoked too if I could get a gig like this…"

"It's Stokes, not stoked," Josie interrupted. "Let me see that thing." She grabbed the papers from Iggy. "So, I guess he's giving us a break this time. Maybe it's a two-fer kind of thing. My half is five thousand. He needs five thousand up front before he will get started. Well, count me out. If Richard wants him back so badly, he can pay the retainer."

"What I don't get is why would Richard throw away money on these quacks? What is he - brain-damaged or something?" Iggy went into the kitchen to get another beer.

Josie continued to read the order. "So it looks like the good doctor will fly to Montana and follow me around for three days and update his report. Great. It's not like I have any choice in the matter."

"Well, whatever you do, don't sign anything, Josie." Iggy announced loudly, walking back into the dining room with a beer in his hand.

"I don't have to sign. The judge ordered it already. It's out of my hands," Josie replied.

"Speaking of signing things – take a look at these signatures." Iggy held up the signature page of one of the documents. "If you didn't know what these guy's names were, there would be no way you could ever figure it out."

Alice took the paper from him. "Weiner's signature is just a check mark and Richard's looks like a Richter scale read-out," she said, handing the paper back to Iggy.

"I noticed the same thing last year when I briefly looked into some of the shenanigans Richard's dad and his buddies were up to years ago," Josie agreed. "I found deeds and documents where it was impossible to tell whose signatures were on them. I figure it gets back to the family motto: 'you can't prove it.' I mean, there's no way anyone could prove that either Weiner or Richard actually signed these things."

"It's called plausible deniability," Alice said. "It's disgusting – even their signatures are part of a ruse."

Alice opened another envelope. "This looks like another motion. She flipped through it again. What? Didn't he just file a motion for custody and child support? Why's he filing another one? You just had a hearing on that."

"Give me that." Josie reached out her hand and took the papers from Alice. "It hasn't been filed. See, there's no court stamp on it." Josie held up the paper and pointed to the right hand corner. "It's just another unfiled document. We've been through this before – remember? It's more bullshit from Weiner."

"Good catch, Josie, I forgot about that. That's just pure bullying and intimidation. It's court-sanctioned bullying," Alice scoffed.

"Why would he do this?" Iggy looked up from his papers. "Doesn't all this cost him a lot of money? What does that attorney make anyway? Your ex has a screw loose." He walked over and opened the door to the living room and leaned in to check on the boys.

"You're right, Alice. This is all bullying and intimidation. They're trying to break me. They figure I'm up here, isolated and broke and he'll just blitz me with legal filings until I start drinking and go off the deep end." Josie walked into the kitchen and came out with two more beers.

"This is the blitz. It's a bombardment of family court nukes."

"Scud missiles more like," Alice corrected her. "You can do better than this, Josie. We'll make your filings lethal – unlike these duds."

"Yeah, but why is he spending this much money? That's what I don't get." Iggy asked again.

"A few reasons, Iggy. First, when it comes to his own private war he will gladly step over a dollar to pick up a dime if he can hurt me in the process. Second, let's look at what he's really spending to do this. Yeah, it costs Richard more to send a bunch of filings over and over but really it's chump change considering the amount of intimidation it buys him." Josie leaned her head back and drank some beer.

"So he has to pay a little extra to ship multiple copies of the same filing – along with a few bogus unfiled documents - all of which could have been sent in one envelope. But when you get one of these things every single day it is so much more demoralizing. That's what this is really about."

"Anyway, what's the plan? I need you guys to help me figure out a plan here." Josie looked at her friends.

"Fight fire with fire," Iggy offered. "It doesn't cost you anything to fire back and Richard has to pay to have a lawyer or paralegal to read through each piece of paper you send them. I say you start sending them something every day. Every. Single. Day. And I still think you should file a motion to counter everything he's doing. He files for less child support, you file for more. He files for more visitation and you file for less. Everything he does you counter him."

"I notice Weiner has a fax number," Alice spoke up. "Josie, you need to get a fax machine and start sending him faxes. That way you don't even have to pay for shipping. You can start faxing and re-faxing your own legal filings every single day. The more pages the better. Obviously it doesn't matter if they've been filed or not. So make up some bogus filings and fax them too. Every single page will cost Richard – they probably charge a couple bucks a page just to receive a fax, and then of course some high-dollar attorney will have to read it all," Alice said brightly. "In fact I have a fax machine I never use – I'll give it to you."

"That's a great idea, Alice." Josie paced back and forth across the dining room. "This is war. I love the idea of faxing Weiner hundreds of pages of documents – and there's no way he can even prevent me. He'd have to turn off his fax machine and then he couldn't do business with anyone else either." Josie and Alice started laughing. "Are we having fun yet?"

"Hey, Paul's asleep – I've got to get home." Iggy opened the French doors to the living room.

"Before I go – something else just occurred to me: I wouldn't worry about this custody evaluation. My bet is that nothing will happen. Nothing will change. Not because this Dr. Stokes likes you better or anything. I don't think anything will change because in order for Richard to get custody this doctor guy would have to reverse his previous decision. Those kinds of guys never reverse themselves. They never go back on what they already decided. It would be like admitting they got it wrong the first time. Guys like that – with PhDs next to their names – those guys never admit they got something wrong."

"Thanks, Iggy. We thought of that too. But still, it's stressful for me. It means I have to spend three days pretending to be the perfect 1950s TV mom. It's total crap. Anyway, you guys are the best legal team I could hope for. I'll see you later."

"And we're the only one you can afford," Iggy said, giving Josie a hug.

"Yeah, that too."

"So, Iggy thinks I need to start filing motions." Josie put Austen and Phoebe to bed and sat back down in the dining room. "Easy for him to say, he doesn't have to go before the judge."

Josie was still traumatized by her last hearing. She'd tried to defend herself and tell the court what really happened in the marriage, and the judge ruled against her on every issue. It felt like she couldn't have done any worse.

"I just keep thinking that if I hadn't said all the things I said in the last hearing that maybe the judge wouldn't have ruled against me on everything. HE GAVE THEM EVERYTHING." Josie emphasized each word. "It was a rout. It was devastating."

"You need an attitude adjustment girlfriend. You're still not in the right frame of mind. One time at my old job my co-workers and I brought a case against our employer. It was heard in federal court and it couldn't have been more lopsided. The company had done so many egregious things and we'd documented all of them. Tim acted as our attorney – pro bono. He was absolutely brilliant. Time after time we went to court and Tim destroyed the sleazy company lawyers. And time after time the court ruled against us. There's no getting around it, it's a corrupt money-driven system. You get all the justice you can afford. It wouldn't have mattered if you'd crawled in there bowing and scraping before the judge. The outcome will be the same regardless of what you say in court. Iggy's right – you should start filing motions. Fight fire with fire," Alice said.

"I used to hear the saying that the best defense is a good offense. I never really understood it. Now I finally get it," Josie said. "I can't get over the fact that Richard is the offender. He hurt our kids. He destroyed our marriage. But when we go to court he immediately goes on the offensive against me and puts me on the defensive. Weiner slandered me the very first time he opened his mouth. I've been playing defense the whole time and I didn't even do anything wrong!"

"Okay, Josie you can turn this around. You need to take the offensive. Keep talking until they tell you to shut up. What are they going to do? Threaten you with contempt? I guess they always have that power." Alice walked into the living room and sat down on the couch.

"I guess you might have to accept that possibility," she suggested. "My sister went to jail for two days once when she refused to hand over a source back when she was a reporter for the local paper. She lived through it just fine. She held to her principles and to this day it's the thing she's proudest of. So, the worst that can happen is they hold you in contempt – for speaking truth to power. I mean chances are they won't. If they started throwing family court litigants in jail every time they talked too much there wouldn't be any room left. Aren't the jails full out there anyway? I heard some places aren't even prosecuting burglaries anymore."

"I heard that too." Josie followed Alice into the living room and sat down in her favorite chair.

"And Iggy's right about Dr. Stokes. That guy won't reverse his prior decision. His ego won't let him. You'd have to be shooting up heroin in front of the kids and having sex on the living room floor for him to even think about reversing his decision. And we all know you're pretty tame. Except for the occasional beer you don't do anything. You won't even smoke a joint with me. Anyway, Stokes will take the job and get his free trip to Montana along with his fat paycheck, and Richard will get nothing. Maybe he'll throw the guy a bone – give him an extra day at Christmas or something." Alice finished her beer and stood up to leave.

"Let every word be an arrow straight into the heart of this corrupt system. Just like your dream, Josie. Write volumes about what really happened. Write it over and over and over. Drown out their lies and manipulations with the truth."

41

Josie rose early each morning to start working on her legal filings. The words flowed out of her and the declarations seemed to write themselves. She found free templates online, along with all the legal forms she needed on a free legal website. She soon realized that lawyers charge hundreds of dollars an hour to download and fill out forms that anyone with a computer can do for free.

She carefully analyzed Weiner's writing style and used it against him. He was fond of bold declarative sentences that accused Josie of being "mentally unstable," or of "alienating the children," or "making false accusations." There was never any substantiating evidence for these bold statements but that didn't stop him from making them. As far as Josie could tell, the objective seemed to be to make outrageous and damning statements presented as facts for which there wasn't any actual evidence, before moving on to less dramatic claims for which he actually had some sort of supporting documentation. Basically, most of Weiner's filings amounted to a lot of standard forms that anyone could fill in, attached to a declaration full of unsubstantiated bullshit.

"Two can play this game," Josie thought to herself as she pulled up the template and started writing.

Once she understood the format, Josie found that writing legal documents was easy and fun. There was no shortage of damning statements she could honestly make about Richard, and unlike Weiner, she often had supporting documentation. It wasn't long before she realized that Weiner was no legal scholar. Richard wasn't paying him for his commanding presence in the courtroom or his nuanced understanding of the law. He was just a hack. A highly paid hack busily sucking up the college funds and helping to destroy the lives of untold families like hers.

Soon she was regularly printing out legal documents of a hundred or more pages, which she then gleefully faxed to Weiner's office. "Bombs away!" She told Alice one morning. "I'm sending a giant scud missile over to Weiner right now! Are we having fun yet?" The women giggled.

"That should wipe the smirk off his face," Alice said.

"Yesterday I received a letter from them telling me that I was no longer allowed to send them faxes because quote 'I used up too much toner!' That only makes me want to send more! Honestly, this is the most fun I've had in ages!" Josie gushed. "Oh and I almost forgot – he also sent me a bogus legal filing that said I was going to be declared a vexatious litigant!" Josie laughed. "I would love to declare him a vexatious litigant but guess what?"

"What?" Alice said.

"It turns out that only pro-per litigants can be declared vexatious! An attorney can harass someone as much as they want and it's perfectly legal!"

"Wow, Josie. Well, I guess that's what we get when the state government is controlled by attorneys," Alice said.

"Bingo!" Josie agreed.

"You know," Alice continued, "I was looking at the Bar association website for La Costa County and surprise, surprise, it turns out the Weiner is breaking every ethical rule they have. It's almost like he used their professional code of conduct as a reverse play book for how to run his practice. I think a complaint to the Bar association is in order. And of course make a copy of the complaint and file it with the court for good measure."

"Alice, that's brilliant! I love it! I'll work on that today!" Josie quickly pulled up the Bar association website on her computer. "Wow, you're right. Every single thing they say that attorneys aren't supposed to do, he's been doing to me! This is his playbook. And guess what else I found out?" Josie asked.

"What?"

"Next week is Weiner's birthday! I can have this filing prepared and have it hit the docket on his birthday! They say that turnabout is fair play – who am I to argue?" Josie laughed again.

⋐ 42 ⋑

Pulling up to the house after dropping Phoebe off at school one morning, Josie noticed a police car in front of the neighbor's house. The neighbors were a young couple with an infant and were the only people on the block who hadn't been friendly to Josie and her family. Josie blamed their cool reception of her and the children on the previous tenants. Since arriving back in Montana, Josie had fired her property management company and had become involved in all of her ownership duties. When she went to the neighbors carrying a baby gift for their newborn, she had apologized again for the previous bad tenants.

She got out of her car and opened the back door to retrieve her groceries. A young police officer approached. "Is something wrong officer?" Josie inquired, wondering whether something had happened to her neighbor or the baby.

"Your neighbor, Mrs. Lombardi, claims that you threatened her and she wants to file a police report. Can you tell me what happened?"

Josie was speechless. Mouth gapping, she glanced over at her neighbor who had retreated to her front porch.

"I'm sorry officer I have no idea what you're talking about. I just returned from dropping my daughter off at school, and picked up some groceries." She motioned to the bags in the back seat.

"Honestly, I'm speechless. I've never been anything but kind and considerate to her since I moved in a few months ago." Josie's heart was pounding and she frantically tried to remember if she'd done something wrong.

Recently she noticed that the neighbors had posted a sign on the tree in front of their house stating that the street in front of their property was their private parking area – despite the fact that it was a public street. She'd also noticed that the husband had several cars and that their family, with only two drivers, took up twice as much space on the crowded street as she and her tenants combined. One of her tenants was upset about it, but Josie had decided not to get involved.

The officer went back to speak to the neighbor, while Josie waited by her car not sure what to do. After her neighbor went back into the house the officer came back to talk to Josie.

"Stay away from them," the officer told her. "Don't engage with them. Don't talk to them. Don't look at them. Don't go on their property. Don't let them on your property. There have been several calls to this residence in the last two years." Josie nodded in compliance and thanked the officer as he left. She grabbed the groceries and locked the car.

"What was that about?" Francine asked. She was just coming out of her apartment when she saw Josie talking to the police.

"I don't know. I'm totally bewildered." Josie shook her head as she opened the front door. Francine followed her in the apartment and watched as Josie unloaded groceries onto the kitchen counter.

"Apparently the neighbor called the police and told them that I'd threatened her. Can you believe it? I'm a middle-aged woman and she's twenty-five - and I'm a threat to her?" Josie said, incredulous. "Coffee?" She turned to Francine.

"Sure, I have time for coffee." Francine got cups down from the cupboard, while Josie filled the kettle.

"They've always been nice to Beau and I, but for some reason they've gotten into it with the tenants in this apartment. I've watched it happen for years now. The last guys before you were actually pretty cool. They kept the music down, and never left beer cans around like a lot of students. My only complaint was when their girlfriends were sunbathing on the front porch all summer in their string bikinis. Beau's eyes nearly fell out of his head. He kept making excuses to go downstairs so he could check them out. But the guys themselves were always cool."

"That's interesting, Francine. I brought them a baby present when we first moved in – and I apologized for the previous tenants even though I really never knew the whole story about what happened between them. My old property manager said they were just a bunch of young guys and had turned out to be bad tenants so he evicted them. It's weird though - this is the first time anyone has ever called the police on me." Josie shivered.

"The cop was great though. He just told me to stay away from them. Not to let them on my property, not to go on theirs. I plan to do exactly what the officer said – totally ignore them." The two women walked into the living room with their coffee.

"For some reason their last name seems really familiar to me." Josie looked at Francine.

"It's probably because her family owns a lot of property around here. They have a real estate company and a property management company," Francine offered.

"That must be it. I was looking for a new management company and I must have seen their name. Good thing I didn't pick them – I didn't like the manager at all."

"This place was so cheap when I bought it years ago. The prices have tripled since then. Maybe the family has a habit of harassing tenants thinking the owners will get sick of it and sell. It sounds ridiculous but I'm sure weirder things have happened," Josie said.

"Also, there's something else I heard once," Francine told Josie. "Her family used to own this building years ago. I think Beau told me that – not sure where he heard it, though." She sipped her coffee.

Josie's eyes widened when she heard that the family next door had once owned her building. "So they have been deliberately harassing my tenants trying to get me give up and sell the place. The management company always told me that it was hard to keep tenants in this apartment even though it's beautiful. Now I know why." Josie shook her head.

"First my ex is busy trying to steal all the property I owned before we even met and now these neighbors are trying to do the same thing. Geez. This stuff is starting to creep me out. I never realized there were so many vultures in the world."

"I'm sorry, Josie. Like I said, they've always been nice to us. They got into it with the other tenants but never with us. We just try to get along with everyone and just try not to get involved with the drama."

"That's good thinking, Francine. I don't blame you. Anyway, I think this officer knows what he's talking about when he says not to engage and I plan to do exactly that."

When Austen ran to the corner to meet Phoebe's school bus the following day, Josie sat on the front porch and watched. Just as he ran past the neighbor's house Mary Lombardi came out and called to him.

"Hi, Austen." She waved at the little blond boy as she held her own infant son. Austen stopped when he heard his name and looked back at his mother for help.

After her encounter with the police, Josie had explained the new rules to the kids. "Don't talk to them. Even if they try to talk to you, just ignore them. Pretend they don't exist. Pretend you don't see them or hear them."

"Kind of like ghosts, right, Mommy?" Austen asked.

"Yes exactly, Austen. Like ghosts. I know it will be hard, but you have to do it. The police said to do it and we have to do what the police say, don't we?" The children nodded in agreement.

"Those neighbors are a certain kind of people. I call them trouble-makers. They like to make trouble for other people. They have their own secret reasons why they like to make trouble, but the reasons don't really matter. What matters is that we never engage with trou-blemakers. We avoid them. We don't talk to them. We don't look at them and we never go near them." Josie emphasized every word of her little speech and the children had listened intently.

Austen stood frozen on the sidewalk, as the neighbor continued to cajole him. Josie mouthed the words "IGNORE HER" and motioned with her hand for him to turn and run to the corner where the bus was just then pulling up.

The neighbor repeated her performance after Phoebe got off the bus, calling after both kids "Hi, Phoebe! Hi, Austen!" The children both looked down at the sidewalk as they walked quickly past the neighbor's house and ran onto the porch where Josie was waiting.

"Good work, you guys! I'm so proud of you both!" Josie whispered, taking Phoebe's backpack from her and opening the door. Out of the corner of her eye she noticed her neighbor scowling at her.

After that, the situation escalated. More cars belonging to her neighbor's family appeared in front of Josie's building, forcing Josie and her tenants to park on adjacent blocks and in the alley. The neighbor continued to call out to her kids whenever she saw them. Josie's tenants complained to her about the parking situation, but all she could do was shrug. She'd inquired about it at city hall and everything the neighbors were doing was perfectly legal.

The neighbors built an open fire pit right next to the property line so that smoke billowed into her windows. They set up power tools on their front lawn and whenever Josie or her tenants went onto the front porch to talk or read a book, the husband walked outside and turned on the power tools just to make noise.

Then one morning a car drove up and a young man got out. He pounded a 'For Rent' sign into the lawn in front of the neighbor's house. A few days later Josie saw a moving van pull up in front of their house. While the neighbors were busy moving, a young woman stomped angrily over to Josie's building and rang her bell. Josie looked out the window and recognized the woman as a frequent visitor to her neighbor's house.

"Can I help you?" Josie opened the door. "You know why they're leaving don't you? You know why? Because of you! They have to leave now because of you!" Josie shrugged and closed the door. She picked up the phone and called Alice.

"You'll never believe it! The bad neighbors are moving! All we had to do was completely ignore them and they couldn't stand it and now they're moving!"

"That's great, Josie. That was good advice that cop gave you. You might want to write a letter to the department and give that guy some kudos," Alice suggested. "Do you remember his name?"

"I don't remember his name, but I remember what he looked like. He was a big guy and I'm guessing he's one of the only black officers in town. I'll totally write a letter. He was awesome! He gave me the best advice ever."

∽ 43 ∽

Richard parked his rental car in front of Josie's house and waited several minutes before getting out. A dark haired woman sat in the front passenger seat talking on her cell phone. She briefly glanced at Josie's house then looked away. Richard got out and walked up to the porch.

The drapes were drawn in the living room and a small suitcase with the kid's clothing sat next to the front door. Josie stood at the window and parted the drapes with her fingers. *That must be Sheila*, she thought. When the kids returned from their visit to California the previous month, Phoebe told her mother numerous stories about her new step-mother.

"Mommy, she drinks wine all the time," Phoebe tattled to Josie while they were playing crazy eights one evening.

"Well sweetie, we drink beer and wine too," she reminded her daughter. "But she drinks wine in the morning, Mommy. I heard you say to Alice that people who drink in the morning have a problem."

"That's interesting, Phoebe. Let's talk about something else. Do you like her?"

"No, Mommy, I hate her. She locked me in my old room in Loranda and she screamed at me. And she said you were stupid and that me and Austen were going to go back to California to live with them pretty soon. Is that true?"

"Hey, Phoebe, hold up there. Did you say she locked you in your room? And she told you I was stupid? That's bad. She's not supposed to do stuff like that. So, why did she lock you in your room? Did you do something wrong? Where was Daddy?" Josie shook her head in disbelief.

"Daddy was at work. And I was good. She just gets mad a lot. And then she yells at us," Phoebe told her mom.

"Wow, that's not good. Just when I think it can't get any worse, it gets worse. Wait just a second sweetie, I'll be right back."

Josie went into her bedroom and pulled a small notebook from the bottom dresser drawer. It was the log book she'd used to document instances of Richard's abusive behavior towards the children. She sat on the bed and wrote down everything her daughter had just told her before rejoining the card game.

"Mommy I hate her and Austen would hate her too but she always buys him a lot of toys so he probably thinks she's nice."

"Listen, Phoebe, she's Daddy's wife now. She's your step-mother. You have to try to get along with her. I read in some court papers that she has kids but you haven't mentioned them. What about her kids? What are they like?"

"I only met one and he's creepy. His name is Brady. He's twenty years old and he dropped out of college and he lives with Daddy and Sheila. He sleeps all day and walks around in his underwear. They gave him the whole downstairs and he plays video games all the time. Her other kids are all older. They live in other states and stuff. She's a grandmother, too."

"Geez, how old is this woman anyway? She has three adult children already?"

"I think she's around your age, Mommy. I heard her say she's forty-two. She had her first baby when she was fifteen. Daddy told me I need to respect her because she had a baby in high school and had to raise him by herself. And I think her kids all have different dads. She said Daddy is her fourth husband. But Brady said he never met his dad. I guess they move around a lot."

"Wow. So Daddy married a woman who has three adult children by different men and the last one doesn't even know his father. And she's been married FOUR TIMES? Nice." Josie picked up the cards and put them into their box. "It's time to get ready for bed Phoebe. Austen's been asleep for over an hour."

Phoebe went into her bedroom to change while Josie followed her and sat on the bed. "Sweetie, there's something important I need to talk to you about." Phoebe sat down next to her mother. "If you ever notice that Sheila is drinking wine please don't get in the car and drive with her. Okay? Do you understand? And don't let Austen get in and drive with her either. Okay?" Phoebe nodded her head.

"From what I've heard so far, it sounds like she doesn't have very good judgment. So please promise me that if you notice her drinking wine please don't let her drive you or your brother anywhere." Josie took her daughter's hands in hers.

"Just tell her that you saw her drinking wine and it's not safe for you and Austen to drive with her. Tell her you will call the police if you have to. Okay? And, as far as respecting her because she had a baby in high school, I have to tell you that I don't agree with Daddy about that. I'm not saying you shouldn't respect her, but that you should base your respect on something worthy of respect. Getting pregnant when you're fifteen is a mistake and it's not something you should respect."

Several minutes passed while Josie peered out the window and recalled her conversation with Phoebe. Suddenly the doorbell rang.

"Austen, Phoebe. Come here. It's time to go. Daddy's here." Josie clapped her hands as she called the children.

"I don't want to go," Phoebe whined. Josie picked up the suitcase and opened the door.

"Hi, Austen! Hi, Phoebe!" Richard bellowed as he tried to push past Josie and enter the house. Josie silently and deliberately blocked him from entering and stepped outside with the luggage.

Phoebe stood frozen in place, with tears rolling down her face. "Here, take this." Josie unceremoniously shoved the overnight bag at Richard without looking at him. "Austen, follow Daddy. Phoebe, sweetheart you need to go."

She took Phoebe by the hand and gently tugged her out the door. "It'll be fine. You'll be back in two days. You'll be in Montana the whole time. You can call me if you want to talk." Josie put an arm around her daughter and slowly walked her to the waiting car.

Sheila stared at Josie with an angry expression as she watched her approach the car with Phoebe. She looked right at Josie's face but Josie never looked up as she gently guided Phoebe around the side of the car and helped her in. Once Phoebe was in the car and the door was closed, Sheila jumped out and stood in the middle of the sidewalk with her hands on her hips, blocking Josie's way.

"How dare you!" She screamed at Josie as Josie put a hand out to introduce herself. "How dare you! This poor man! Do you know what you've done to him?" Josie flinched and stepped backwards as Sheila lunged towards her, swinging both arms wildly. Richard quickly ran over and grabbed Sheila by the shoulders, holding her just out of arms reach of Josie.

"What? What are you talking about? Oh my God – were you trying to hit me?" Josie took another step back as she stared at the angry woman, whom Weiner had told the court should be raising her kids. They couldn't be more different. Josie was tall and slender, while Sheila was short and pudgy. Josie was trying to be polite and introduce herself, while Sheila was trying to rip Josie's face off.

"Quite frankly I'm flabbergasted, Richard. This is the first time I've had some woman try to take a swing at me. Unbelievable. Anyway, I don't have time for this school yard bullying, and it's against my policy to engage with angry people," Josie stated flatly as she turned to walk away.

"Let me go!" Sheila screamed at Richard as she struggled to free herself.

"Just get in the car Sheila, she isn't worth it." Richard coaxed Sheila back into the car before running around and jumping into the driver's seat. The car jerked forward before making a U-turn and taking off. Austen's face was pressed against the window and Josie waved him goodbye. Iggy came down the sidewalk towards Josie, gesturing towards the departing car shaking his head. Laughing, he walked over to Josie and gave her a hug.

❧ 44 ❧

The temperature was a perfect seventy degrees with a slight breeze and the city below them was in full bloom. Josie could just barely make out the roof of her house from the top of her favorite trail even though it was partially shrouded by leafed-out maple and locust trees.

"Another beautiful day in paradise," Josie put her arm behind her head and leaned back on the warm rock, soaking up the sun. Francine took a drink from her water bottle and smiled. "It's amazing how things work out," Josie said.

"I bought that building sight unseen years ago when I was working as a ship engineer and now I'm living there with my kids and having a great time. I never planned it that way. It's so great that you and Beau are right upstairs and Iggy is next door. It's like the universe made a perfect little place for us to land in our time of need."

"It's a beautiful building, Josie. You mean you never laid eyes on it before you bought it?"

"No, but my parents were living here then. My dad found it – he talked me into investing some of my money up here. My mom never liked it – it's too old for her taste. Fortunately for me it turned out to be the perfect time. I would never have bought it if it wasn't for my dad."

"What did your folks do here?" Francine asked.

"My dad taught at the university. We weren't rich but we were fine until I was about fourteen. Then something happened and my dad lost his job. To this day I don't know the details. Suddenly we went from the genteel poverty of a university professor to actual poverty as my dad drove all over the state looking for work. Unless you have a good business or you're tenured with the university, this is a tough place to make a living."

"Tell me about it," Francine agreed. "Beau and I left good jobs in the Bay Area and we're barely making it up here. But you can't beat the quality of life. We still think it's worth it."

"I left when I was seventeen and I never thought I'd come back here to live - at least not full time," Josie said.

"Looks like you've done okay for yourself, Josie. Beau and I are so happy you guys are downstairs now. It's so nice having a family here. We love our apartment. One of these days we plan to buy a place but we're not in any hurry. We came up here to visit an old friend of Beau's and she convinced us to stay. It helped that the university accepted me as a grad student." Francine stood up and stretched. "Anyway, I think life is what you make it." The two women headed back down the trail.

Josie followed her friend down the mountain, trying to match Francine's long athletic stride. Bright yellow mule ear flowers leaned into the narrow trail, brushing against Josie's bare legs. Suddenly Francine stopped and turned around.

"Check it out, Josie – mountain goats!" Francine pointed to a clearing half way up the mountain where three large animals with thick white fur and slender curved horns grazed quietly, indifferent to their presence.

"Wow, it's great to see that there are still mountain goats on this hill. We used to see them all the time." Josie angled her cell phone towards the goats and took a few pictures. "Last week I was walking on the river trail and I spotted a bald eagle. Random wildlife sightings around town make up for a lot as far as I'm concerned," Josie said as Francine nodded in agreement.

"Of course the Bay Area is supposed to be paradise, too..."

"Well, this place is full of Bay Area ex-pats," Francine said. "In fact, we know quite a few people from there – I think we should have a party, Josie!"

"I was just thinking the same thing. I'll host it. I'd love to start meeting more people up here. Most of the people I knew twenty years ago have left town. You and Beau have such interesting friends – could you invite some of them?" Josie said.

"Sure, most of my friends are artists. They'll never turn down free food and drinks. We should have a theme – maybe a costume party." The women made their way back to the parking lot at the bottom of the trail.

"What about a retro party? I have a whole collection of vintage dresses. We can put Beau in charge of the music. What do you think?" Francine opened the passenger door and got in.

"I love it. I don't have any vintage dresses but I know a place I can get one. The kids love to play dress-up. How about next weekend?" Josie asked.

"I'll take you to my favorite store, Josie – everything is vintage and it's all really inexpensive. I love going there." Francine beamed at Josie as they drove back to their neighborhood.

"Oh, I forgot to tell you my news!" Josie said excitedly. "I went to the university and took the grad school exam yesterday. It was pretty spur of the moment. I'm supposed to get health insurance for myself and the kids so I figured I would try to get in to grad school."

"Really?" Francine looked at Josie. "How did you do?" She asked.

"They graded it while I was waiting. Apparently I did pretty well – I hope well enough to be accepted. I already sent over my application a couple weeks ago – all I had left was to take the test." Josie pulled up in front of their building and Francine was poised to get out.

"What department?" She asked.

"I've decided on the art department – painting actually. It was a hobby for of mine for years. I worked overseas a lot and I always drew and painted when I had time. After I came back to live in the states I took classes part time at San Francisco university. It was a couple years before I got married. Somehow I ended up with enough units for anther bachelor degree. I never thought in a million years I end up applying to grad school for painting."

Francine was surprised. "I thought you were an engineer."

"I am. Or I was. It's a long story. But basically I don't have my license anymore and even if I wanted to go to grad school for engineering, this university doesn't have an engineering department." Josie shrugged.

"Well I know almost everyone in the art department. I could tell you stories. Do you have any work you can show me?" Francine asked.

Josie pulled up in front of their building.

"That's a sore subject, Francine. I have photos of my best work and I gave those to the department. I stored everything in my garage in Loranda and I had an agreement with my ex that I could come back during summer break and get it. It was mostly my artwork and a few boxes of photos and some books. Anyway, when the kids came back from spring break they told me that their step mother had gotten rid of all my stuff. I asked my ex about it and he just shrugged. I guess my mother was right – I should have taken everything when I left. Anyway, best not to dwell on it." Josie and Francine got out of the car.

"Could you invite some people from the department to the party?" Josie asked.

"Sure, I can do that. I'll warn you right now – even though your scores are high, for some reason they hardly ever admit locals into the grad program there. I've had so many artist friends apply and get rejected. I was accepted but I ended up leaving before I got my degree. In the end it hasn't mattered though, I've done better in my art career than a lot of the graduates I know."

"Thanks for the warning, Francine. It's definitely something to take into consideration. Anyway, let's go vintage dress shopping tomorrow!" The women parted and went into their respective apartments.

When the weekend came Beau went down to Josie's apartment early to set up speakers in the dining room and hook up his computer to play party tunes. Francine and the kids hung paper lanterns across the porch and decorated the living room with colorful murals they made on long rolls of newsprint. Alice brought over a case of beer and Iggy helped Josie make enough pizzas to feed a crowd.

The guests began arrive and Beau sat down at the piano and arranged some sheet music. Joseph, the skinny blond boy from the yellow apartments next door, stood next to him holding his clarinet. Josie wore a black sleeveless 1950's party dress with a full skirt and heels. She introduced herself to several artist friends of Francine's as well as a few grad students from the art department.

"You ready?" Beau turned to his young neighbor. Joseph nodded. "Let's hit it!" They played a collection of old Broadway show tunes they'd been rehearsing for the occasion. The crowd stopped to listen.

"Wow, Beau! Francine said you'd be in charge of the music but I never thought we'd have a live performance!" Josie was headed into the living room with a fresh bottle of wine.

"Don't get too excited. We only have a few tunes. We're just trying to kick things off. I'll crank up the party music after we're done." People flowed from the dining room into the living room and out onto the porch. Peals of laughter and hearty banter floated above the music. Iggy expertly worked the crowd and Alice slow danced with Tim. Josie stood in a corner with her arms around Austen and Phoebe.

"Are you guys having fun?"

"Yes, Mommy!" They answered in unison.

"This is the best party ever!" Phoebe yelled above the music.

"Are you happy we moved here?" Josie asked.

"Yes!" Phoebe yelled while Austen nodded in agreement.

Josie felt happy and grateful. She'd been blown off course but had ended up in a better place. Her kids were doing well, they'd all made friends and she was finally able to see a future for herself beyond the litigation.

Iggy came over and handed her a glass of wine. "You good?" he asked.

"Yes, I'm good."

"Great party! Everyone's having fun!"

"Guess what?" Josie leaned in close to Iggy.

"What?"

"I got my letter from the university today! They offered me a spot in the graduate program!" She smiled at Iggy and he gave her a fist bump.

"This calls for a celebration, Josie – I have a bottle of champagne at my place. I'll be right back." Iggy went next door to get the champagne while Josie danced in the living room with her kids.

∽ 45 ∾

Josie ran along the narrow rim of a vast canyon until she reached a wide level opening framed by several large boulders and a bent and twisted tree. The sun was high and the sky was clear. Her body was moist with sweat and her heart was pounding. Stopping to catch her breath, she leaned against a boulder and gazed into the abyss below her. A low voice spoke from behind, startling her.

"The world is full of houses. Let it go and another will come. The world is full of money. Let it go and more will come. Reclaim your name. Reclaim your identity. Of this there is only one. It is more valuable than the house and more important than money."

Josie turned around and saw a massive mountain lion with large yellow eyes and smooth tawny fur crouching on the rock above her. Silently and without warning, he sprang into the air and landed on top of her. She fell backwards as her arms flailed above her head.

Floating above her body, feeling as light as a wispy cloud on a summer day, Josie watched the scene unfurl in slow motion. The lion stood on top of her, pinning her shoulders under his massive paws. He bent his head and roared repeatedly into her chest until the vibrations filled her heart. Then, just as suddenly, he released her and leapt back to his perch on the rock.

Josie returned to her body and lay on the warm ground with her eyes closed. Slowly, she stretched out her limbs and took a deep breath, feeling more alive than ever. The voice spoke again:

"Let your words roar into the hearts of others."

She opened her eyes and the lion was gone. Josie picked herself up and turned back towards the canyon. She looked down at her hands and a book appeared. Amazed, she brought it closer and ran a finger over the gilt letters that spelled out her name. She began to open it when an eagle swooped down out of nowhere and grabbed it in his talons. The eagle flew high above the canyon as Josie watched. As he soared towards the sun he released the book from his grip. In an instant the sky exploded with words. Millions of words filled the sky.

Josie opened her eyes and stretched as much as she could in her cramped seat. She was on the early flight from Montana and had fallen into a fitful sleep. Dr. Stokes had come to Montana two weeks earlier to follow Josie around and she'd turned herself into the wholesome TV mom with the immaculate house once again. He'd followed her to the skating rink where Austen was on the peewee hockey team, then watched as she made afternoon snacks for the kids before presiding over Phoebe's homework. She was still appalled at the unnecessary expense and the intrusion into her life, but she was a lot more relaxed the second time around.

As predicted, Stokes didn't go back on his previous decision – and Josie knew it probably had less to do with her parenting skills than it did with his own ego. Iggy was right – Stokes wouldn't reverse his previous decision because he'd be admitting he'd made a mistake the first time around.

Josie was on her way to California to attend her divorce trial. She had just received Stokes report and the accounting report the day before her trial and had briefly flipped through them. There was no way to outrun this legal and financial tsunami and she wasn't even going to try. She was going to let the universe blow her off course and she felt free.

She thought about the dream she'd just had. Why fight over a house? The world is full of houses. Why fight over money? The world is full of money. The only thing she cared about was having the kids stay with her and she knew that was unlikely to change.

❧ 46 ❧

Josie arrived at the La Costa County courthouse early on the morning of her trial. She stepped off the shuttle and walked briskly down the still-empty streets looking for a coffee shop. Resembling a homeless lawyer with her wrinkled suit, her worn back pack stuffed with trial binders and her purse overflowing with a change of clothes, she headed to a corner coffee shop.

Dropping her heavy pack on a seat near the window, she ordered coffee. She checked her messages and smoothed her suit before sitting down. "I'm here, not to worry." Josie left a message for Alice, who was getting already to go to work in Montana. "It's early. I have an hour to go through my binder. I'm tired from the travel. I'm feeling kind of trashed. One way or another I hope this is finally over today." She hung up and rummaged through her pack before pulling out a thick brown legal binder with clips at the top. Sipping her coffee, she slowly picked up each page and examined it before going on to the next.

The day brightened and the sidewalks began to fill with people. She looked across the street and spotted Richard parking his car. He got out and checked his reflection in a store window before dropping coins into the meter. *Always the narcissist*, thought Josie. Her phone rang. "Hi, yes I'm fine. I'm starting to get my second wind. Richard's here. He just walked by on the other side of the street. He's alone." Josie sipped her coffee while talking to Alice. She'd been worried that Richard would bring a regiment of Bain family members to the trial. At the very least she figured he'd bring his new wife.

"He's such a weenie - I thought for sure he'd bring his attack dog wife with him for further intimidation. Guess I was wrong. He has Weiner, his pit bull attorney, though." Josie started to laugh. "At least I'm going into this thing in a decent mood. I have to go now – people are starting to line up at the courthouse door." Josie hung up and gathered her things. She swung her pack over her shoulder and went to join the line.

A heavy woman in a pink dress called the court to order while the judge walked in and took his seat. A tall heavy man with glasses, Judge Wood scanned the courtroom while the clerk called Josie's case.

"Adam Weiner here, representing Richard Bain." Weiner spoke softly and the judge asked him to repeat himself. "Adam Weiner, representing Richard Bain, the Petitioner in this case, Your Honor."

The judge looked sternly at Josie. "I'm Josephine Bain. I don't have an attorney," she stated.

"From my experience it's usually the most litigious person who ends up at trial without an attorney," the judge said gratuitously. "Usually the unrepresented party at trial outspent the other side and then ran out of money."

Josie was taken aback by the Judge's hostile and prejudicial comment. "Actually, Your Honor, I need to set the record straight on that. It is the petitioner who has out-spent me at least three to one. I ran out of money last..."

The judge cut her off abruptly, waving his hand at her. "I have your filing here, Ms. Bain. With or without an attorney you will need to be sworn in and begin your testimony."

"Okay, no problem," Josie said. She stood and approached the clerk, bringing a pen and notebook with her to the witness stand. She held up her right hand and swore to tell the whole truth and nothing but the truth before taking her seat.

"So do I just sort of pretend there's a lawyer here asking me questions?" Josie looked up at the judge.

"Yes, just begin talking. Give your testimony. You're the lawyer and the witness."

"Okay. Well, since I need to tell the whole truth I will begin by telling the court that this entire divorce was caused when Mr. Bain abused our children and the county child protective services told me to protect them..."

"Strike that from the record. Strike that entire statement," the judge instructed the court reporter. "I won't let that stand."

Josie had been sure that Weiner would jump to his feet and object with his usual dramatic flair, but instead it was the judge who shut her down.

"With all due respect Your Honor, it is my sworn duty to tell the whole truth and I intend to do just that." The judge scowled at her as she continued her testimony.

"It's true that I'm not employed at the moment. I became unemployed after I took medical leave during my last pregnancy and Mr. Bain decided to sabotage my career by hiding my license renewal notice. He knew that since I was at home caring for an infant and a four year old, I was unlikely to remember my renewal date without seeing the notice." Josie paused and looked at Richard. "It's also true that Mr. Bain wouldn't have the job he currently holds had my former boss not hired him as a favor to me. But since no good deed ever goes unpunished when you're dealing with Mr. Bain, he decided to repay me by depriving me of my livelihood. It was pure malice, Your Honor." Josie stopped and glanced at the judge.

"Where is this going Ms. Bain? Where are you going with this testimony?" The judge was testy.

"We're having a trial about support issues and property issues, Your Honor. I'm explaining to the court that I am currently not employed in my former profession due to the deliberately harmful actions of Mr. Bain. I am also explaining to the court that he has doubled his income in the last three years solely because of my benevolence towards him. I am benevolent and he is malevolent: I want that on the record." The judge nodded and waved his hand at Weiner who was about to object.

"I could go on for hours, Your Honor. I could talk about the fact that all the property in Montana was mine years before I ever met him and that I now stand to lose some, if not all of it. I could talk about the fact that I always acted in good faith by fully funding my retirement plan while Petitioner deliberately stopped funding his plan after our marriage because he evidently planned all along to divorce me. Let's just face facts, Your Honor, Mr. Bain is a bad actor. He has acted in bad faith in every possible way – including abusing our innocent children for his own selfish ends." Josephine stopped as Weiner objected.

"I have no doubt I will pay dearly for my mistakes but after it's all said and done, I will pick myself up and move on. I can out-work, out-smart and out-earn Mr. Bain a thousand times over." Josie paused.

"What I won't soon recover from is the way I've been treated by our justice system throughout this process. To put it simply, the person with the most money wins. The person with the best lawyer wins. The person with no money loses. The person with no lawyer loses.

Now I ask - how is that justice, Your Honor? What is the point of a justice system that can't protect the powerless from the powerful?

Mr. Bain has used the system to bully me, Your Honor. This has been nothing less than court-sanctioned bullying. When I finally started to fight back Mr. Weiner threatened me with vexatious litigant charges. I thought we were supposed to have equal justice under the law. The judges in our family courts are almost all former divorce lawyers. They all socialize together and they hate pro-per litigants like me. I've been impoverished by this incestuous system and it will take me years to recover.

Like most Americans. I thought our justice system was supposed to be impartial - but then I learned that our previous judge is Mr. Weiner's tennis partner. How is that okay, Your Honor? I was told that as long as they don't discuss our case then it's all just fine. But of course I can't prove one way or another whether they ever discussed our case - can I, Your Honor? Mr. Weiner is one of the most expensive attorneys in La Costa County – but as you saw yourself it isn't due to his commanding courtroom presence. He squeaks like a mouse and you had to ask him to speak up. Having read all his filings I can also safely say he isn't paid top dollar because of his fine legal mind. So I ask you - what else can it be Your Honor? Pay to play, perhaps?"

"I object!" Weiner sprang to his feet. "This is pure speculation and character assassination! I object in the strongest possible terms to any suggestion of malfeasance by my law firm! If Ms. Bain has evidence of malfeasance by my firm let her show it to the court!"

Josie had really gotten a rise out of Weiner – he was so agitated that he actually raised his voice loud enough for the judge to hear him.

"Witness is refrained from speculating about malfeasance on the part of opposing counsel. Any further testimony on the subject will result in contempt of court charges. Are we clear, Ms. Bain?" The judge spoke harshly and Josie shrank down in her seat as he glared at her.

"I suggest we retire to my chambers and settle this thing. We can work out a judgment and both parties can sign. Do you agree Ms. Bain?" The judge asked impatiently.

"I refuse to sign anything, Your Honor. I refuse to sign any document that results from such an unjust system." She paused and bit her lip. "I want you to rule. I want you to put your name on this injustice. I want you to own this. I want the court to own this. I know the consequences of my choice, Your Honor. I know you will most likely give him the marital home, as well as properties I owned years before I ever met him. I know he will get half of my retirement fund and I fully understand I may never have another Christmas vacation with my children while they are young. I am at peace with my decision. There will be other houses. There will be more money. I will celebrate Christmas with my kids in July if need be." The judge looked down at her, his face red with anger.

Undeterred, she continued. "There is only one thing that I want and it is the one thing that Mr. Bain can never have. I want my identity back." She paused again. "I want my maiden name restored. I will never again go by my married name."

She glanced at the Petitioner's table and saw Richard's shoulders slump as he heaved a heavy sigh. She hadn't expected that. She expected his smugness. She expected his delight at what he would without doubt consider her total capitulation. She hadn't expected that taking back her maiden name would wound him, but it had.

The judge banged his gavel. "The court adopts the accounting report prepared by Simons accounting firm which awards the marital home as well as the non-retirement investment accounts to Mr. Bain. The court clerk will now sign Ms. Bain's name on the quit claim deed awarding the marital home to Mr. Bain."

The clerk shuffled through some papers on her desk, located the quit-claim deed and signed it. Then she typed the order giving Richard all the money in their brokerage account.

Josie flinched, she hadn't seen that coming. She'd received the accounting report just hours before her flight and hadn't had time to thoroughly read it. Once onboard the plane, she'd flipped through the pages and stared at the charts and tables of numbers - but she didn't know the first thing about accounting and couldn't interpret it. She hadn't even been able to figure out what the bottom line was as far as how the accountant had divided up the marital property. Instead, she was fixated on one thing: looking at the report, she realized for the first time that the accountant had almost the exact same address as Weiner's law firm. She'd dealt with the accountant via emails which also included Weiner, and a couple of times the accountant had made three-way phone calls between herself, Josie and Weiner – but this was the first time Josie recalled actually seeing the physical address of the Simons accounting firm.

She'd faxed the report to Tim as soon as she received it and called him on her way to the airport. He'd told her that the report was supposed to have arrived at least thirty days before trial. To make matters worse, Weiner had handed Josie the appraisals for the Montana and Loranda properties on the day of the trial and she'd barely had time to glance through them before the proceedings started. She noticed that they'd been prepared weeks earlier and was shocked at the values, but the last minute inundation of documents had happened so fast that she hadn't had time to process it and include it in her testimony.

"The court orders that Ms. Bain's retirement fund be divided by the Simons accounting firm and that both parties equally bear the cost of that accounting."

"The court further orders that the minor children live with Ms. Bain during the time when school is in session and be returned to father during all school vacations."

Josie flinched again and let out a little gasp when she heard the judge say "all school vacations," knowing it included Christmas and Thanksgiving.

"Lastly, the Court restores Ms. Bain to her former name of…" The judge flipped through some papers. "Josephine Blume." He banged his gavel again and abruptly left the courtroom.

Josie stepped down from the witness box and walked over to her table. Her head was spinning as she stuffed her court binder and her jacket into the backpack. It had been a gut-wrenching experience and she felt ill. She wanted to ask someone what just happened but there was no one to ask. Did the judge really give Richard the house and all the money from her marriage? She felt dizzy and sat down to get her bearings.

"Congratulations, Josephine Blume you're a free woman." Josie spun around and saw Iggy striding towards her holding a bouquet of flowers. "What, Iggy … when did you…?" She stammered. Before she could stand, Iggy leaned over and put his arm around her and gave her a hug.

Over on the petitioner's side, Richard's face was red with anger. The veins on his neck were pulsating and his voice was several decibels too loud for the nearly empty courtroom. "I was supposed to get full custody! You said the court favors married couples!" He started to yell. Weiner grabbed his client by the elbow and led him away, trying to calm him.

"Come to think of it, I think this is more in order." Iggy made sure to catch Richard's eye before he took Josie in his arms and kissed her.

Josie kissed him back then smiled. "So, uh what was that? I thought we decided…"

"That we're not doing this? We did. But I couldn't resist rubbing a little salt in his wound." Iggy winked at her as they both looked over at Richard's angry face, glowering at his fast talking attorney.

Still half embracing, Iggy and Josie burst out laughing at the same time. "It's too funny, Iggy. He'll never be happy." Josie wiped a tear from her eye.

"Hey – check it out - a tear – you actually shed a tear Josie. I'm proud of you!" Iggy told her in a low voice.

"Don't get too carried away Igman. It's a tear of joy from having this whole thing over with finally."

"Hey, let's get out of here. I haven't been in San Fran in twenty years – you mind if we head over for lunch? I have a car." Iggy checked the time on his phone.

"Lunch in the city? Sounds good to me." Josie heaved her pack onto her shoulder and the two friends walked out of the gloom of the dimly lit courthouse into the bright afternoon sunlight.

∽ 47 ∾

On the evening of her first gallery show Josie felt buoyant and cheerful. She'd invited all her friends to her house for a party after the art opening was over, and she'd left the gallery early to prepare for her guests. Austen and Phoebe were still at the opening with their friends and Iggy had volunteered to bring them back later.

Josie sat down on her living room sofa and took off her heels. She thought about the uncanny timing of her show – five years to the day since she'd forced Richard out of the house. It was a pure coincidence – she hadn't planned it that way. Glancing around the room, she looked at the artwork on the walls and the photos of the kids - building snowmen, ice skating and inner tubing on the local river. She had built a good life for them, and for herself.

After her trial, she and Iggy had spent three days in the Bay Area visiting friends and family before returning to Montana. Things had happened quickly during the trial and she knew that Weiner had pulled a fast one, but it wasn't until she was back in Montana that she had time to put the pieces together.

Looking through the accounting report after she returned home, she realized that there was little likelihood that a complicated financial situation with multiple properties and other investments such as hers and Richard's would result in one party getting all the marital property and the other party getting nothing. It would be nearly impossible for Weiner to have gotten her share down to exactly zero without significant malfeasance. When she showed the Montana appraisals to a prominent local realtor he had laughed out loud. He told her that none of her properties had ever been worth anywhere near what the appraisals claimed they were worth.

It then became clear what had happened: Weiner had violated the court rules by talking privately to the accountant, whose office was across the hall from his. The accountant had provided Weiner with the exact number that the appraisals had to add up to in order for Josie's share of the community property to be zero. Then Weiner went to work getting the right appraisals to make it happen. He'd already stalled and delayed the trial knowing that the Bay Area real estate market was declining – a subject which he'd blogged about on his firm's website - but then he went a step further and hired a local appraiser to produce what Josie was later able to determine was an artificially low appraisal of the couple's marital home in Loranda. In this way Weiner minimized Josie's share of the marital home so that Richard could 'buy' her share for the lowest possible price.

As if that wasn't bad enough, Weiner also found a crooked appraiser in Josie's hometown to prepared artificially high appraisals on all of Josie's Montana properties in order to artificially inflate Richard's undeserved share of those properties. Even though she'd owned her properties prior to her marriage, she hadn't kept the rental income in a separate account and had unknowingly given Richard a legal claim to some of their value. The net result of Weiner's malfeasance was that Richard's share of Josie's property appeared to be worth far more than Josie's share of the marital home.

To make up the phony balance, the accountant's report then awarded Richard the couple's investment funds, which were worth tens of thousands of dollars. Working hand in glove with the crooked appraisers and the unethical accountant, Weiner had successfully brought Josie's share of all the marital assets down to zero. It was all so perfect. In order to pull off the scam Weiner had made sure that Josie got the report and the appraisals at the last possible minute – giving her no time to figure out what had happened.

Of course Weiner knew that Josie would have grounds for an appeal because he'd violated court rules by not providing the documents at least thirty days before the trial, but he also knew that appeals were costly and that if she lost she'd have to pay Richard's legal fees. In addition, he knew that Josie was broke after years of non-stop litigation and that in any case, appellate courts usually uphold the lower courts. Gaming the property trial against a destitute pro-per litigant was as close to a sure bet as he could get, and to Weiner it was a gamble worth taking.

Josie understood what she was up against and couldn't afford to take a chance on an appeal. Still, in the weeks following the trial she did what she could. First, she gathered evidence against both appraisers and filed complaints in Montana and California with the respective licensing boards. The complaint against the California appraiser went nowhere, but she was pleased when the Montana appraiser lost his license a few months later.

Next, she filed a complaint with the board of accountancy in California against the Simon's accounting firm. She knew her complaints against the accountant were likely to be futile, and they were, but she felt compelled to do what she could to fight back against the endemic corruption she'd discovered.

The thing that made the system so easy to game for Weiner was the fact that the burden was on Josie to prove that he had talked privately to the accountant about her case. Over the course of her divorce, Josie had discovered the truth about the justice system. Weiner had filed motion after motion and had stalled and delayed the settlement in order to get more for his client by timing the market. He had consistently lied to the court about Josie and when she finally found the courage to fight back he threatened her with being a vexatious litigant – charges that he himself was immune from because of his law license.

He played tennis with the judge and Josie was supposed to believe that they'd never discussed her case. His office was across the hall from the accountant and again, Josie was supposed to believe that they'd never discussed her case.

After dealing with the dishonest appraisers and the accountant, Josie belatedly began to examine the role played by the trial judge. Prior to her experience in family court, Josie naively assumed that judges considered evidence and made judgments. In reality, both of Josie's judges merely rubber-stamped reports prepared by the highly-compensated court experts which she and Richard had been forced to hire.

But what if the court expert was corrupt? What if they used the wrong data or methodology? She recalled watching as the trial judge had quickly flipped through the accounting report which he had also just received the morning of the trial. She knew there hadn't been time to read through it and at best he'd only glanced at the concluding paragraph which awarded all of the marital property to Richard.

Late one night, a few weeks after the trial was over, Josie bolted straight up in bed with the sudden realization that even if the judge had only read that one last paragraph of the report he should have known something was wrong. An experienced judge would have known that it was impossible for the accountant to have come to such a neat and tidy one-sided conclusion.

In fact, Josie had looked up the record of her trial judge before hand and had been comforted to find out that prior to becoming a judge he'd been a highly-regarded federal prosecutor and had been instrumental in rooting out white collar crime. Surely, Josie thought, such a man would see through Weiner's nefarious actions and give her a fair trial.

As it turned out, she couldn't have been more wrong. In a harsh and unprovoked attack, the judge opened the proceedings by letting Josie know what he thought of pro-per litigants. He had leaned forward in his chair and sternly told her that in his experience people like her were usually the ones who'd vastly outspent the other side, only to run out of money for the trial. When she tried to correct him he'd shut her down with a wave of his hand. Caught off-guard by his hostility, Josie was immediately put on the defensive and struggled to regain her composure for the rest of the trial.

Months later she finally made sense of his behavior. His unprovoked attack was an attempt to discredit her so he could assuage his own role in the unsavory proceedings and justify his decision not to question the accountant's report. The judge had taken a page from Weiner's playbook: the best defense is a good offense. As a former federal prosecutor, the judge would have known that the accountant had cooked the books as soon as he saw at the bottom line. Instead of protecting Josie and administering justice as he was sworn to do, he'd openly flirted with the accountant and good-naturedly waved the requisite voir dire background questions for her while she smiled and crossed her long slim legs in the witness stand. At best he was complacent, at worst he was corrupt.

Alice had been right all long – there was to be no justice in Josie's case and the best she could hope for was to bust a few kneecaps on the way down. Josie had found out first hand that the family court is a corrupt, incestuous, money-driven system that has nothing to do with justice and everything to do with enriching the unethical people who work in the system. The burden on Josie to prove that Weiner had violated the rules was an impossible burden and he knew it. Her excessively litigated, several-year-long divorce could have been shut down quickly if the court had leveled the playing field by ordering Richard to pay some of Josie's legal fees - but that would have been bad for business. Josie realized that the single most important goal of the divorce industry and the family court is not to administer justice. Rather, the single most important goal is to perpetuate the income streams of the people who work in the system.

The divorce had been devastating and disheartening, and after doing what she could to fight back, Josie made a determined effort to put it behind her. In the months after the trial she'd thrown herself into her graduate school studies and into her children's many activities. Austen played pee wee hockey, while Phoebe played in the youth orchestra and regularly landed speaking roles in the acclaimed children's theater in their hometown. She packed her days with activities and most nights fell into bed, exhausted. Occasionally the anger and bitterness crept into her thoughts late at night and she made a point of counting her blessings.

Money was always a worry, but Josie forged ahead and cultivated a belief at all would be well. She used business acumen that she didn't know she possessed and made an advantageous deal with a developer who wanted to buy one of her properties. She took over the management of her properties and several of her tenants told her she was the best landlord they'd ever had. She was fair with everyone and worked hard to see that her tenants were safe, comfortable and satisfied with their units.

She taught college classes full of students from all over the world and never missed the weekly get-together at Zippy's bar with the other grad students in her department. Even though they were all much younger than her, several of the other grads had become friends. Before long, she and her children had their own Montana tribe.

Iggy had moved across town and Paul was enrolled in private school, but they'd remained close. The two families continued to spend most Friday evenings together, sharing meals and laughs. Francine and Beau had purchased a fixer-upper in one of the hippest areas of town but they were still frequent dinner guests at Josie's place.

During her first semester in grad school, Richard once again filed a motion for reversal of custody and Josie had felt the old despair and weariness flood back. The motion was set to be heard during finals week and she couldn't believe that she would have to drop everything and once again gear up for court.

Then something unexpected happened and Richard finally hit a road block. Josie's knowledge of Richard's life post-divorce was filtered through the children, and whatever bits of information her friends were able to glean from his and Sheila's social media accounts. Her friends kept her updated on the latest photos posted by Sheila and they had a few laughs about the fact that she had gained at least fifty pounds since her marriage to Richard and that she'd quit her high-paying job as soon as the ink was dry on her marriage license. Especially hilarious to Josie was the fact that Richard couldn't even dredge up his usual phony smile as he scowled at the camera in all of the photos.

Richard's life really began to spin out of control shortly after he filed his last motion. Usually so careful not to abuse the kids in front of witnesses, he'd been seen hitting Phoebe in the parking lot of a Loranda grocery store and an onlooker not only called police but had stayed with Phoebe and given a detailed statement when the they arrived. For her part, Phoebe had dutifully reported to the officer that she'd refused to get in the car or allow her brother to get in the car because Sheila had been drinking and was in the driver's seat at the time. Phoebe told the police that Richard tried to force them into the car and had hit her when she wouldn't comply and that Sheila had run around to the passenger seat as soon as she heard the police were on their way.

Josie was outraged when she realized Sheila was trying to drive her kids around after she'd been drinking, and that Phoebe was once again hit by her father, but she also saw an opportunity. This time Richard had dropped ammunition behind enemy lines and Josie - now a seasoned and battle-hardened family court litigant - knew just what to do with it.

Josie's response to the court filing, which included copies of the police report, was searing and powerful. She reminded the court once again of his abuse of the children and his disregard for their welfare. She was surprised when her case was unexpectedly reassigned to a different courtroom and was relieved that the hearing was rescheduled for after her finals week at the university.

Despite Alice's repeated warnings that the courts are hopelessly corrupt and that judges routinely close ranks and support each other's decisions, Josie was filled with optimism about the new judge in her case. She thought that a different judge – one who didn't play weekly tennis games with Wiener - would see through Richard's machinations and come down hard on his mistreatment of the children. She was gleeful at the thought that Richard would not only lose his latest motion for full custody, but would end up with supervised visits as well.

Sadly, her optimism had been unfounded. Yes, Richard did lose his motion for reversal of custody, but everything else stayed the same. Josie had appeared at the hearing by phone and listened as Weiner explained away the police report and made light of the incident in the parking lot. She had no doubt that Richard was at the petitioner's table wiping phony tears from his eyes throughout the proceedings.

At age twelve, Phoebe was tall, strong and athletic. Her experience in the parking lot that day had emboldened her and she'd refused to get in Richard's car during subsequent visitation exchanges. Richard had made one brief attempt to manhandle Phoebe the first time she refused to go with him, but he let go of her as soon as he noticed Josie taking cell phone video. Phoebe hadn't spent time with Richard in months, and at one point told her father that she was going to change her name as soon as she was eighteen and would never see him again.

For her part, Josie was careful to abide by the court order and dutifully brought both children to the visitation exchanges, despite the fact that Phoebe routinely refused to go with her father. Josie steered clear of any interaction between Richard and the children, but was ready to take video or call the police if she noticed anything amiss. Richard never missed a chance to glower at her when he caught her eye, but she ignored him.

Austen often complained to Josie that he didn't want to go either, but she always told him he had no choice. She'd overheard Phoebe tell her brother that when he was big he could also refuse to see their dad, but until then he'd have to deal with it.

Josie thought about how things had finally caught up with Richard as she changed into jeans and uncorked a bottle of cheap champagne. By all accounts his marriage to Sheila was falling apart and his kids wanted nothing to do with him. He'd gotten all the property, but by fighting back hard Josie had made sure that it cost him dearly. Josie knew that life's what you make it, and she had made hers stimulating and fulfilling while Richard had made his into a war zone.

She continued getting ready for the party. She got the beer out of the fridge and put it in the ice chest in the living room. She put a CD in her battered old boom-box and set two trays of hors d' oeuvres on the dining room table next to a vase of fresh flowers. The house was decorated with balloons and streamers and Josie had hung several of her recent paintings in the dining room and hallway. She'd had a hard time choosing what to put in her show so this party was a way for people to see the rest of her work.

It was getting late and the gallery walk was over. The guests began to arrive at Josie's house for the after party. "Come in," she called out as Francine and Beau opened the door, followed by one of the adjuncts from Josie's department and several grad students. Iggy arrived next while their kids stayed outside making snow angels and reveling in the great benign blizzard that had just drifted into town.

Iggy put an arm around Josie as she handed him a glass of champagne and poured another for herself. "You've come a long way since I met you, babe. I'm proud."

"Thanks Iggy. I'm proud, too. We have a great life up here – thanks in no small part to my friends." Josie motioned to Francine and Beau and the others. The two friends clinked glasses.

"A long time ago someone told me that revenge is a dish best served cold, but now I realize that in fact, the best revenge of all is living well and being happy." Josie smiled and drank her champagne.